99p

RELISH
GREATER
MANCHESTER
& CHESHIRE

Original recipes from the region's finest chefs

First Published 2011
By Relish Publications
Shield Green Farm, Tritlington,
Northumberland NE61 3DX

ISBN 978-0-9564205-5-8

Publisher: Duncan L Peters
General Manager: Teresa Peters
Marketing and Design: Ria Parkin
Principal Food Photography: Adrian Gatie
Additional Food Photography: Tim Green
Cover: John Fraser/Marketing Manchester
Account Manager: John Bunyan
Proof Assistant: Jack Bamber
Printed By: Balto Print Ltd, Stratford,
London E15 2TF

All recipes ©the restaurants

RELISH
PUBLICATIONS.CO.UK

004
CONTENTS

006
CONTENTS

DESERTS

The "Bees Knees" Cheesecake

Mojito

Trio of Chocolate

Raspberry and White Chocolate
Cheesecakes

Dark Chocolate Delice with Amaretto Ice Cream,
Toasted Pistachios and Espresso Foam

Strawberry Bavarois with Strawberry Parfait

Steamed Cherry Pudding with Cherry Brandy
Custard

Summer Pudding

Dunham Massey Rhubarb Fool

Manuka Brulee

RESTAURANTS

INTRODUCTION WITH ANDREW NUTTER

Andrew Nutter is among the most exciting and innovative of the new breed of celebrity chefs to hit the culinary circuit.

An award-winning author and proud Mancunian, he showcases the region's produce to its full potential. Andrew is at the forefront of modern British cuisine, not only here in the UK at his Rochdale restaurant but also abroad in South Africa, Australia, New Zealand and America, where his TV shows are now broadcast. A true ambassador for Greater Manchester and Cheshire!

And on the eighth day God created Man, Chester and food, glorious food. At one stage food in Greater Manchester and Cheshire was looked down upon, with run of the mill eateries using processed food and serving up bog standard meals, but now, boy o' boy, it's standing proud as a proper destination for foodies across the land.

Having been involved in the Northwest's restaurant dining scene since the tender age of 21, I have seen first-hand the change in chefs' attitudes to finding and sourcing great produce, and it's amazing to see the calibre of great chefs that this region is now producing.

What is interesting is quite literally the sheer range of amazing restaurants, bakers and small boutique delis that are all adding to the current revolution that is putting Greater Manchester and Cheshire in the spotlight. Michelin standard chef Michael Caines' arrival in the Northwest has added a great deal of clout to the hotel restaurant dining scene, with two fabulous eateries at the Abode Chester and Manchester.

Diversity and sheer range of eateries is one key factor, with owners' attention to detail and the chefs pushing the boundaries with their sourcing of local ingredients highlighting this region's food to its full potential.

Once our only foodie claim to fame was the humble Eccles Cake and a lump of Cheshire Cheese, now it's the region's eateries that are taking centre stage and getting both national and international acclaim.

Take, for example, Mr Maverick himself Rob Owen Brown at the Mark Addy – a great riverside location for his nose to tail eating experience. Perfect on a sunny afternoon, and yes that does happen occasionally in Manchester! The gourmet delights of Stuart Thomson at the chic Harvey Nichols Second Floor Restaurant in Manchester city centre, or the hidden gem of Aumbry tucked away in my home town of Prestwich. Looking for food with that Italian touch perhaps? Well venture across to Chris Johnson's Ramsons restaurant in Ramsbottom for a truly eclectic experience.

The styles are so varied across the region and this book is the perfect tool for you to use, enjoy and explore. Little did I know when I was the new kid on the block in Rochdale in 1993, that I would be part of such an exciting industry. Flick through the pages of this book, the bold and vivid prints catching your eye, it's food porn at its finest. Be inspired and try the recipes for yourself – but better still, go visit the restaurants (no washing up to do that way) and take yourselves on a culinary journey. After all, you don't need to be a Nutter to try out the restaurants in this book, but you'd be an utter nutter not to.

Andrew Nutter

010
1539
RESTAURANT & BAR

The Racecourse, Chester CH1 2LY

01244 304611
www.restaurant1539.co.uk

1539 Restaurant & Bar is a fabulous, glass-fronted eatery with magnificent, panoramic views across Chester Racecourse, which creates a perfect setting in which to enjoy contemporary British cooking. The restaurant is named after the year that horse racing first began in Chester, back when the Lord Mayor of the city was one Henry Gee, hence the term gee-gee's referring to a horse.

Head Chef, Rob Brittain, is passionate about the provenance of food and takes great care in sourcing the best local, seasonal produce from farmers and producers who care as passionately about food as he does. Vale of Clwyd beef, Goosnargh chicken and duck, morning-fresh vegetables from Cheshire farms and herbs from their very own herb garden all feature on the menu.

1539 has won a string of awards, most recently the prestigious Best Large Restaurant award at the 2011 Chester Food, Drink & Lifestyle Awards - and also the Silver award for best use of local produce.

Above the restaurant is the newly extended Roof Lounge and terrace- a totally unique venue, offering luxurious alfresco dining during the summer months. It can also be hired out for private entertaining; birthdays, weddings and special occasions, or simply a superb setting for a pre or post dinner drink.

Above the restaurant is the newly extended Roof Lounge and terrace – a totally unique venue, offering luxurious alfresco dining during the summer months

COLD PRESSED GOOSNARGH CHICKEN & HAM 'PIE', PEA VINAIGRETTE, ROCK SALT PASTRY CROUTE

SERVES 8

 Mâcon-Charnay, Cuvée à L'Ancienne
France (Burgundy)

Ingredients

1 ham hock
3 chicken legs
50g parsley (chopped)
1 onion
2 carrots
1 leek (finely chopped)
1 bay leaf
2 sprigs of thyme

Rock Salt Pastry Croute

200g puff pastry
1 egg yolk
sprinkle of Cheshire rock salt

Pickled Girolles

150g fresh girolles
1 medium sized banana shallot (finely diced)
50ml white wine vinegar
75ml Great Ness virgin rapeseed oil

Garnish

200g peas
1 curly endive (pickled and washed)
1 punnet pea shoots

Method

For the chicken and ham

Put the ham hock in a pan of cold water and bring to a gentle simmer, skimming off any impurities that come to the surface. Peel and roughly chop the onion, carrot and leek (saving 100g of the white part of the leek for later) and add them to the pan along with the bay leaf and thyme when the liquid is simmering and clear. Cook the ham hock until you can easily remove the smaller bones. Put the chicken legs into a tray, season with salt and pepper, cover tightly with tin foil and place in an oven at 180°C for about 30 minutes or until the juices run clear.

Sweat the finely chopped leek in a little oil until it is soft but without colour. Allow the chicken and ham to cool slightly and pick the meat, discarding any skin, fat and bones. Mix the cooked leek, chopped parsley, flaked chicken and ham together and season with salt and pepper.

Using two layers of clingfilm stretched on to a work surface, put about half of the mix across the middle of the clingfilm and roll into a tight cylinder, twisting at the ends to create a sealed cylinder. Put a few small holes in the clingfilm to get rid of any excess air and twist the ends a couple more times. Roll quickly in another piece of clingfilm to stop any juices getting out and refrigerate overnight.

For the pastry

Roll the puff pastry out to about the thickness of a £1 coin and cut into 15cm x 2cm strips, then lay it onto a greaseproof lined baking tray. Egg wash each strip, trying not to allow any to run off the sides. Sprinkle with Cheshire sea salt, place another piece of greaseproof paper on top and cover with another tray (to prevent the pastry rising). Bake in an oven at 180°C for approximately 20 minutes or until crisp and golden.

For the pickled girolles

In a hot pan, add a splash of vegetable oil and quickly add the girolles mushrooms. Fry them until nearly cooked, then add the diced shallot and toss through the mushrooms for 20 seconds. Add the white wine vinegar and reduce slightly before adding the rapeseed oil. Warm slightly, then take off the heat and allow to cool. These can be done up to a week in advance and stored in an airtight jar in the fridge.

For the garnish

In a food processor, pulse the peas slightly to break them down without pureeing. To make the pea vinaigrette, mix the peas with the girolles, add the oil and season.

To serve

Assemble as in the picture, adding the pea vinaigrette and curly endive to finish.

ASSIETTE OF CHESHIRE PORK WITH CREAMED CABBAGE, CRISP BELLY, PAN FRIED FILLET, SAGE & APPLE FAGGOT

SERVES 8

*Monthelie AC Domaine Roulot 1999
France (Burgundy)*

Ingredients

Belly
1kg pork belly (whole with skin removed)
500ml dry cider
salt and pepper
half the vegetables (from the cheek ingredients below)

Faggot
450g pork mince
50g suet
1 Granny Smith apple (grated)
2 onions (finely chopped)
2 tbsp sage (finely sliced)
125g breadcrumbs
salt and freshly ground black pepper
200g crepinette

Cheek
8 pig cheeks (with sinew removed)
4 carrots (peeled and chopped)
2 onion (peeled and chopped)
4 sticks celery (chopped)
1 bulb of garlic (cut in half)
150ml white wine
1tsp tomato puree
500ml veal stock

Method

For the belly

Put half of the vegetables on the bottom of a deep baking tray with some pork bones (if you have them) and put the pork belly on top. Season with salt and pepper and pour the cider over. Cover with tin foil and cook in the oven at 160°C for 3-5 hours depending on the thickness. You should be able to put a knife through easily.

When the pork is cooked transfer it to a clean tray with greaseproof paper and top it with another tray with a plate and a weight on top of that to press the belly. Place in the fridge and leave overnight. Drain the cooking liquor and save for the pig cheeks.

For the cheeks

Season the pig cheeks and put into a hot pan, colouring on both sides, then remove from the pan and set aside. In the same pan put the rest of the vegetables and caramelise, add the tomato puree and cook for a few minutes. Deglaze the pan with the white wine and reduce by half. Put the cheeks back in the pan with the vegetables, add the veal stock, cover with a piece of greaseproof paper, put the lid on, turn the heat down low and cook for about 2 hours until tender. Keep checking that the liquid level doesn't get too low (top up with a little water if needed).

For the faggot

Sweat the finely chopped onions and allow them to cool. Mix the pork mince, cooled onions, sage, breadcrumbs, grated apple and suet. Season with salt and pepper and fry a small bit to check the seasoning.

Cut the crepinette into 3 inch squares. Roll the pork mince into 8 equal sized balls, wrap in the crepinette and set aside in the fridge until needed.

To assemble

Put the pork belly and pig's cheek braising liquors into a pan and reduce until it reaches a sauce consistency.

Place the faggots onto a baking tray and put into a preheated oven at 180°C for 20 minutes, or until golden brown all over and cooked in the middle. If they colour too soon, turn the oven down and cover with foil.

Trim the pork belly, cut it into 8 equal portions and seal in a hot pan (fat side down) until golden brown, then turn and colour each side. Place in the oven for 5- 10 minutes with the faggots.

To serve

We serve this dish with mashed potato, apple puree and creamed cabbage. Drizzle with the pork sauce.

'MOJITO' WHITE RUM PANNA COTTA, LIME SHORTBREAD, MINT SUGAR

SERVES 12

🍷 *Coteaux du Layon, Chateau la Variére Loire, France*

Ingredients

Panna Cotta

375ml double cream
750ml whipping cream
360g sugar
17g leaf gelatine
white rum to taste

Mint Sugar

100g caster sugar
60g mint leaves

Lime Shortbread

500g plain flour
200g caster sugar
400g butter
1 egg yolk
2 limes

Method

For the panna cotta

Mix the two creams together and warm about 150ml in a pan, adding the caster sugar to dissolve it.

Soak the gelatine in a bowl of cold water to soften. Drain the gelatine well and add it to the warm cream and sugar to dissolve.

Strain the warm cream into the rest of the cream and add white rum to your taste.

Pour the cream mixture into individual moulds and put into the fridge. Allow to set over night.

For the mint sugar

Put the sugar in a food processor with the mint leaves and blend until all the mint and sugar is bright green. Put to one side in an airtight container.

For the lime shortbread

Cream the butter and sugar together, add the lime zest and egg yolk. Mix in the flour, being careful not to overwork it. Wrap in clingfilm and let it rest in the fridge for an hour.

Roll the shortbread mix out to about 5mm then cut into 3cm squares.

Put onto a baking tray with greaseproof paper and bake at 160°C for 12-15 minutes. When they are cooked, take out of the oven and sprinkle with caster sugar while still warm. Allow to cool.

Peel and segment the lime and mix with some finely sliced mint leaves.

To serve

Loosen the panna cotta by placing the moulds in warm water. Then turn out onto the serving plate.

Sprinkle with mint sugar, put some of the lime salsa on top of the panna cotta and serve with the shortbread.

020 ALDERLEY RESTAURANT

Alderley Edge Hotel, Macclesfield Road, Alderley Edge, Cheshire SK9 7BJ

01625 583 033
www.alderleyedgehotel.com

The 3 AA rosette Alderley Restaurant – part of the Alderley Edge Hotel in the most exclusive of Cheshire villages - has splendid panoramic views over the Cheshire Plain and a well-earned reputation for exceptional fine dining. The original Elizabethan-Gothic style building was built in 1850 for one of Manchester's wealthy industrial elite. Today it is owned by the J W Lees family and managed by Ahmet Kurçer, whose Lifetime Achievement Award from county magazine Cheshire Life recognised his personal contribution to the Manchester and Cheshire hotel and restaurant industry.

The award-winning hotel, with its beautiful, private, manicured gardens, offers a superb choice of 50 rooms and suites, with services tailored to match the needs of guests who are there for pleasure, business, private dining, corporate entertaining, celebration functions, weddings, conferences, meetings or one of the year's special gourmet events.

The professional team behind the lounge bar and restaurant makes dining an exceptional experience. Head Chef Chris Holland specialises in using fresh produce from local suppliers for his classic British dishes with high-end modern twists. And his menus, with innovative 'sous vide' specialties, have become known for their hallmark of simple but imaginative cooking and clean flavours that are each allowed to stand out individually. With support from an extensive, award-winning list of over 500 wines, they offer an unsurpassed opportunity for truly sumptuous fine dining.

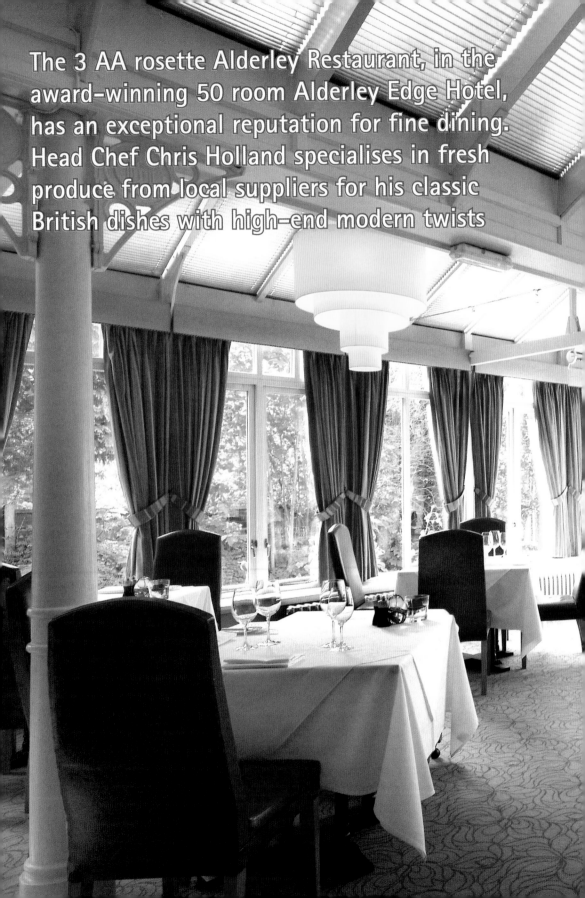

The 3 AA rosette Alderley Restaurant, in the award-winning 50 room Alderley Edge Hotel, has an exceptional reputation for fine dining. Head Chef Chris Holland specialises in fresh produce from local suppliers for his classic British dishes with high-end modern twists

FLAVOURS FROM THE SEA "HOT & COLD", SHELLFISH BUBBLES, AIOLI AND CHERVIL

SERVES 4

 Pouilly Fuisse, Louis Latour

Ingredients

Fish

4 fresh langoustine (blanched and peeled)
2 hand-dived scallops
4 small mullet portions (vacuum sealed)
½ orange (for seasoning)

Ceviche of Prawn

200g King Prawns – split into 3
transglutaminase (meat glue)

Shellfish Bubbles

1litre water
10g alginate
500g intensely flavoured shellfish stock
30g calcium lactate
2 tbsp dill (chopped)

Pernod and Orange Jelly

900ml orange juice
200ml pernod
1g saffron
20g fennel seed
5 tbsp sugar
4g agar-agar

Aioli

½ chilli (deseeded)
2 cloves garlic
½ tsp salt
pinch of saffron
1 egg
200ml first pressed olive oil
2 tsp lemon juice
2 tbsp hot water
pinch of white pepper

Garnish

100g crab mayonnaise
picked chervil

Method

For the ceviche of prawn

Dust a sheet of clingfilm with the meat glue. Lay wafers of king prawn on the clingfilm, making sure they all touch, and dust the top with meat glue. Then, using a meat mallet, flatten this out as thinly as possible.

Refrigerate overnight so that it glues together.

Vacuum pack and Sous-Vide at 58°C for 10 minutes. Refresh and cut out into 15cm discs.

Season with lime, dill and sea salt.

For the shellfish bubbles

Start by mixing the water and alginate together by whisking on low for 10 minutes until slightly thickened. Separately, mix the stock, lactate and dill together then, using a measuring spoon, drop this mix into the alginate water, forming a sphere. Take out and rinse.

These spheres can be heated when you serve the dish.

For the pernod and orange jelly

Mix all ingredients aside from the agar-agar and reduce to 500ml. Then add the agar, simmer and set.

For the aioli

Gently warm water with saffron to infuse.

In a blender, whisk the egg yolk, saffron-infused water, garlic and chilli. Slowly add the olive oil until it emulsifies. Season with lemon juice, salt and pepper and pass through a sieve.

To assemble

Cook the mullet portions at 50°C for 8-10 mins, then pan-fry.

Sear the scallops and blanched langoustines then season with orange juice. Place shellfish bubbles in boiled water to heat up.

To serve

Place the carpaccio of prawn at the bottom of the plate. Quenelle the crab mayonnaise onto the carpaccio of prawn and build the dish with the other ingredients as in the picture.

Place the bubbles on last. Garnish with chervil and serve.

TASTING OF SPRING LAMB, HOT TOMATO TERRINE, OLIVE CRUMBLE, BASIL CROQUETTE

SERVES 4

 Beaune Premier Cru,
J Drouhin

Ingredients

Lamb

1 x 200g Cannon of lamb (vacuum packed, cooked at 58°C for 18 minutes)
1 small shoulder lamb confit (seasoned and pressed)
200g lamb sweetbreads (blanched and peeled)
100g thinly sliced lambcetta (lamb breast cured and smoked)
spray-dried tomato powder (to dust sweetbreads)
200ml reduced lamb jus
250g black kalamata olives (dried for 24 hours and crumbled)

Hot Tomato Terrine

800g over ripe tomatoes
25g basil
2 cloves garlic
100ml white wine
100ml light lamb stock
3½g agar-agar
8 tomatoes (peeled, filleted and seeded)
baby basil leaves

Basil Croquette

350g dry mashed potato
125g choux paste
5 tbsp basil (finely chopped)
1 clove garlic (roasted)
salt and pepper
50g herb breadcrumbs

Method

For the lamb

Crisp up wafers of cured lamb between 2 trays (180°C for 15 minutes). In a hot pan, roast off the lamb confit until crisp on both sides. Add cannon of lamb and quickly seal and season, then place on a wire rack to rest. Roll the sweetbread in tomato powder and pan roast until crisp. Season.

For the hot tomato terrine

To make a jelly, blend the tomatoes, basil, garlic, white wine and lamb stock together and leave to drip overnight through muslin. Use 400ml of this liquid to hydrate 3.5g of agar. Bring this mixture to the boil and simmer for 2 minutes (the excess tomato liquid can be used for a chilled tomato consommé).

Then using an 8cm flexible, rectangular mould, layer the tomato fillets, jelly and basil in alternating layers and set in refrigerator. The terrine is heat resistant to 80°C.

For the basil croquette

Combine the mashed potato, choux paste, basil, garlic, salt and pepper together and roll into small balls. Coat these in the herb breadcrumbs and fry at 175°C for 3 minutes.

To assemble

Serve with English peas (blanched), samphire (blanched), baby carrots (confit with smoked dressing) and asparagus (blanched).

To serve

Butter the vegetables and add to a plate. Spoon a little olive crumble onto the crispy lamb and the tomato terrine and assemble as in the picture. Drizzle with reduction of lamb juice to finish.

'BUTTERED SCONE' ICE CREAM WITH TEXTURES OF CHESHIRE STRAWBERRIES AND ELDERFLOWER

SERVES 4-6

 Laurent-Perrier Rose Champagne

Ingredients

Scones

(makes about 15 scones)

450g self raising flour

150g unsalted butter

75g caster sugar

pinch of salt

2 whole eggs

enough milk to make up to 275mls with the eggs (approx 200ml)

Buttered Scone Ice Cream

(makes about 2 litres)

300g scones

600ml double cream

500ml milk

12 free range, local farm egg yolks

100g caster sugar

75g salted butter

2 pinches of salt

Strawberry Spherification

175ml strawberry puree

20g icing sugar

¼ tsp citric acid powder

5g calcium lactate

Strawberry and Elderflower Cloud Foam

260ml strawberry puree

100ml elderflower cordial (use a good 100% elderflower cordial)

10g powdered egg white

4g Xanthan Gum

Elderflower Jelly

350mls elderflower cordial

250mls water

3¼g agar-agar

3½ sheets gelatine (soaked in cold water until soft)

tartaric acid powder

Method

For the scones

Pre-heat the oven to 190°C.

In a mixing bowl, crumb together the flour, butter, sugar and salt. Add enough of the egg and milk mix to create a fairly sticky dough (It may not need all of the liquid but this can be used to glaze the scones when baking). Roll out the dough on a lightly floured surface to the desired thickness and cut to the desired shape. Brush the top of the scones with the glaze and bake for approximately 15 minutes or until golden brown on the base of the scones.

For the buttered scone ice cream

Place the scones, cream and milk into a heavy-bottomed saucepan and bring to the boil. Allow to infuse for 2 hours then strain. Place the liquid back onto the heat to scalding point. Whilst this is heating, cream the egg yolks and sugar together in a mixing bowl. When the liquid reaches scalding point, pour onto the yolk mixture, constantly stirring to prevent scrambling. Place back onto the heat and cook, constantly stirring, to 82°C or until the mixture coats the back of a spoon. Remove from the heat and add the butter and salt, stir to mix in. Allow custard to cool and then churn. Freeze in the desired shape.

For the strawberry spherification

Make sodium alginate water as for the shellfish bubbles mentioned in 'Flavours from the Sea'. With a stick blender, combine the strawberry puree with the icing sugar and the acid powder then blend in the calcium lactate. Using a spherical measuring spoon, drop spoonfuls of the strawberry mixture into the alginate bath and allow to sit for approximately 5 minutes. Very carefully remove the liquid spheres from the bath and drop into clean, cold water to rinse.

For the strawberry and elderflower cloud foam

Using an electric whisk, whisk together the puree and cordial until a foam starts to form. Mix together the egg white powder and the xanthan gum and add to the liquid. Whisk vigorously until a dense foam is produced.

For the elderflower jelly

In a heavy-bottomed saucepan, bring the elderflower cordial, water and agar-agar to the boil. Add the soaked gelatine and mix to dissolve. Strain through a fine sieve and place in the desired mould. Chill until set. Cut into desired shape and roll in granulated sugar and tartaric acid powder.

To serve

Serve as in picture using the scone crumbs, Cheshire strawberries, wild elderflowers, freeze-dried strawberries, strawberry puree and Cheshire farm clotted cream.

030
AUMBRY

2 Church Lane, Prestwich, Manchester M25 1AJ

0161 798 5841
www.aumbryrestaurant.co.uk

A umbry opened in late 2009 headed up by husband and wife team Laurence Tottingham, Mary-Ellen McTague and their business partner Kate Mountain. The restaurant, at the heart of Prestwich village, 10 minutes from Manchester city centre, is housed in a tiny, converted Victorian cottage.

The intimate dining room and cosy lounge create a warm, relaxed atmosphere.

Laurence and Mary-Ellen both started their careers at Sharrow Bay Country House Hotel, Ullswater, and after spending a year working in the States, they took positions working at the Fat Duck in Bray. They spent 4 years working for Heston Blumenthal before returning home to the North West, initially to work for Paul Heathcote and Ramsons before opening Aumbry with Kate in October 2009.

The chefs at Aumbry seek out the best that the region has to offer in terms of raw ingredients and create dishes that aim to showcase this produce. Using a combination of the very traditional - taking inspiration from historical cookery - and the very latest science and technology, Laurence and Mary-Ellen create dishes of deceptive simplicity. Quality raw produce is paramount to the Aumbry team, and cooking it with care and understanding to bring out the best of each ingredient is their ultimate aim.

Their efforts haven't gone unnoticed as Aumbry won Restaurant of the Year at both the Lancashire Life Awards and Manchester Food & Drink Festival in October 2010, just 12 months after opening. The team are not resting on their laurels though and, after extending the kitchen, they have their sights set on consolidating their achievements so far and further exploring the wealth of fascinating historical British dishes.

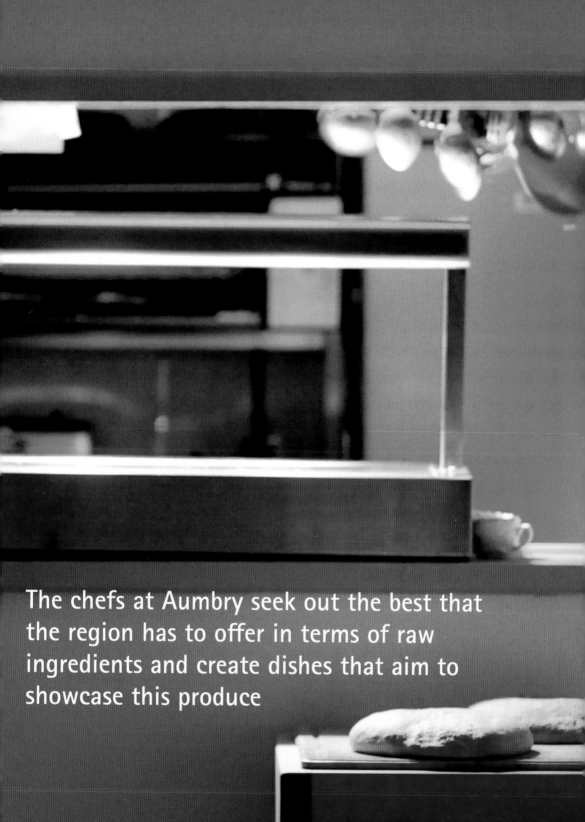

The chefs at Aumbry seek out the best that the region has to offer in terms of raw ingredients and create dishes that aim to showcase this produce

SMOKED MACKEREL, POACHED RHUBARB AND MUSTARD CREAM

SERVES 1

🍷 *Chablis Le Grand Bois,
Grand Chaume, 2008*

Ingredients

Smoked Mackerel

1 x large (350-450g) mackerel (filleted)
60g salt
40g sugar
¼ bunch dill (chopped)
oak chips
2 wire racks

Poached Rhubarb

2 sticks rhubarb
100ml Grenadine
25ml Cointreau

Mustard Cream

50g wholegrain mustard
10g Dijon mustard
150ml double cream
10ml lemon juice
20g caster sugar
2g salt

Method

For the smoked mackerel

Use a box or container to smoke in - we use 2 deep gastronorm trays but it can be anything fireproof that is large enough to hold the 2 wire racks and that can be sealed shut.

Fillet the mackerel, and mix salt, sugar and dill to make a cure. Place the salt cure in the bottom of a non-reactive tray or container, then place mackerel fillets onto the salt, flesh side down. Cover and place in the fridge for 24 hours, then remove from the salt cure and rinse in cold water for 1 hour. Pat the mackerel dry with kitchen paper then submerge in olive oil for 24hrs. To smoke the mackerel, assemble the wire racks; a pan of oak chips; a tray of ice and the smoking box. Lay the mackerel fillets skin side down on one of the wire racks and heat the oak chips in a pan until smoking hot, then set alight. Allow the chips to flame for a minute then extinguish by covering with a lid, then quickly place the pan of smoking chips in the bottom of the smoking box, followed by the other wire rack, then the tray of ice, then the wire rack of mackerel. Cover immediately and close tightly so that no smoke can escape (tin foil around the join of the 2 boxes is very effective at sealing the smoke box shut). Leave to smoke for 45 minutes. Remove the mackerel and place into olive oil for a further 24hrs.

For the poached rhubarb

Peel the sticks of rhubarb and cut them into even sized rectangles, approx 4cm x 1cm.

Mix the grenadine and Cointreau together then either seal in a sous vide bag with the rhubarb and poach at 60°C for approx 30-40 minutes or until just cooked through, or place all ingredients in a saucepan and poach very gently until cooked but still firm. Chill and refrigerate until needed.

For the mustard cream

Whisk all ingredients together until it can be formed into soft peaks, or is thick enough to coat the back of a spoon, and store in the fridge until needed.

To Assemble

Remove the flesh from the mackerel fillets, either side of the backbone. Place a spoonful of mustard cream and a few pieces of drained, poached rhubarb onto a plate. Place the mackerel on top of the rhubarb and serve.

Chef's tip

We like to serve this dish with a piece of the toasted rye bread as seen in the picture.

PLAICE WITH OYSTER PUDDING AND FENNEL

SERVES 6

 Sancerre Michel Girard
2010

Ingredients

Plaice - 1 per person (filleted)

Fish Stock

fish bones
200ml white wine
1 banana shallot (finely sliced)
3 black peppercorns
½ star anise
bay leaf

Oyster Pudding

200g plain flour
100g suet
5g salt
75ml cold water
clarified butter
1 oyster per pudding
1 50ml/2oz pudding basin per person
fish stock (warmed up and infused with a sprig
each of parsley, chervil and tarragon, then
strained through muslin)

Fennel Puree

2 bulbs fennel
75g butter

Method

For the fish stock

Remove eyes and gills from the fish and roast until an even golden colour all over, then sweat the shallots and star anise in a large saucepan. Deglaze the roasting pan with the white wine then tip all into the saucepan along with the shallots. Cover bones with water and add the peppercorns and bay leaf. Bring to the boil, then skim and reduce the heat to a simmer. Simmer for 20 minutes then take off the heat and leave to stand for 1 hour. Strain through muslin, reduce by about four fifths or to taste.

For the oyster pudding

Mix the dry ingredients together in a bowl then add the water slowly, bringing the dough together to a smooth ball. Leave to rest for an hour, then roll out to 3mm thickness. Cover and leave to rest for a further hour. In the meantime, chill the pudding basins in the freezer then brush with clarified butter. Chill and butter once more, ensure that every surface is well greased in butter. Cut out circles of pastry that are slightly larger than the basin to line the puddings, then cut smaller rounds for lids. If you need to re-roll the pastry to have enough lids, then rest again for an hour. Press the circles of suet pastry evenly into the pudding basins, eliminating any air pockets as you go. Set aside in the fridge whilst you prepare the oysters.

Shuck the oysters, retaining all the juices. Strain the juices to remove any bits of shell then wash the oysters twice in the juice. Drain the oysters on kitchen paper, then strain the juice again. Add some of the oyster juice to the reduced fish stock to taste. Place an oyster in each pudding, then fill with sauce to about two thirds full. Dampen the pastry lids with a wet pastry brush then place on top of the puddings, crimping the edges together with a fork to seal. Trim any overhanging pastry with a sharp knife, then cover and freeze until required.

For the fennel puree

Slice the fennel as thinly as possible on a mandolin then either seal in a thin layer in a vacuum pouch, together with the butter and place the bags into boiling water (weighed down with a pan or plate to prevent floating), or sweat the fennel in the butter in a wide saucepan until soft. When cooked, transfer to a food processor and blitz until smooth. Pass through a fine mesh sieve then chill until required.

To serve

Cook the puddings on a pan of simmering water for exactly 20 minutes. Cook the Plaice fillets to an internal temperature of 42°C, ideally in a water bath set to 50°C. Drain on kitchen paper and season with salt and lemon juice. Warm through the fish sauce and fennel. Arrange the pudding, fish, and fennel puree on the plate. Garnish with chervil powder and oyster leaf.

ALMOND CRISP DESSERT

SERVES 6

🍷 *Malbec Dulce Naturale Jean Bousquet*

Ingredients

Chocolate Sorbet

50g cocoa
115g caster sugar
85ml glucose
500ml water

Chocolate Mousse

90g 70% Amedei chocolate (chopped or in pistoles)
125ml whipping cream
22g sugar
20g egg white
40g egg yolk

Almond Crisps

75g icing sugar
50g gluten free flour
50g unsalted butter (melted)
50g egg white
candied or sugared almonds

Griottine Cherries

24 griottine cherries
500ml liquor

Method

For the chocolate sorbet

Place all ingredients into a saucepan and simmer over a low heat for 15 minutes. Then weigh the sorbet mix, adding water to bring total weight to 750g (to compensate for any water that has evaporated off during cooking). Blitz with a hand blender, pass through a fine mesh sieve and churn. Store in freezer until required.

For the chocolate mousse

Bring half of the cream to the boil then pour over the chocolate to melt it, stirring until smooth. Whip the other half of the cream to soft peaks then set aside in the fridge. Whip the sugar and eggs together on full speed for 10 minutes, or until quadrupled in volume and quite stiff, then fold the melted chocolate gently into the whipped eggs. Then carefully fold in the whipped cream. Transfer to a piping bag and set aside in the fridge until required.

For the almond crisps

Whisk the melted butter into the icing sugar and flour, and then whisk the egg whites until they begin to froth. Then whisk this into the batter. Pass and chill for an hour before use. Spread onto a silpat (we use a semi-circle mould but you can do any shape you like) and sprinkle with crushed pieces of sugared almond. Bake at 140°C for 5-7 minutes, checking and turning the tray every couple of minutes, until golden.

For the griottine cherries

Place cherries and liquor into a saucepan and set alight. Allow to flame off, then shake the pan and relight a couple of times to ensure all alcohol has burned off. Strain the cherries and leave to drain for a few minutes, then place the cherries onto a silpat or non-stick baking parchment to dry under hot lamps, in a purpose-made drier or in the oven at 60°C until semi-dried (just starting to wrinkle). Place the liquor in a saucepan and reduce to a syrup then leave to cool. Then cover and set aside until required.

To serve

Take a small amount of cherry reduction and drag down the centre of the plate. Snip the end of the piping bag neatly to leave a 1cm diameter opening and pipe the chocolate mousse neatly onto the plate, diagonal to the cherry syrup. Place a tuile upright behind the mousse and place cherries on top. Then pipe further layers of chocolate mousse on top of the cherries. Place another tuile in front of the mousse to hold in place and pipe two neat mounds of mousse at opposite sides of the plate. Stick a broken piece of tuile upright in one, and flat on the other for the sorbet. Place a scoop or rochet of sorbet onto the tuile base and serve.

040
CITY CAFÉ AT THE MINT HOTEL

1 Auburn Street, 1 Piccadilly Place, Manchester M1 3DG

0161 242 1000
www.citycafe.co.uk

As one of Manchester's most up and coming restaurants, City Cafe sets the standard with its simple yet innovative cuisine. The philosophy is a simple one, but it works. The team of award-winning chefs skillfully and carefully prepare the food from locally sourced, quality ingredients to give their customers the very best of what is in season. City Cafe's à la carte menu changes seasonally and the Market Menu changes twice a week, using the best market ingredients to ensure both choice and quality, and all at exceptional value.

The service in City Cafe is classically and professionally balanced with a friendly, home-from-home atmosphere. All guests are treated rightfully as VIP's. City Cafe is part of the Mint Hotel Chain and has critically acclaimed restaurants available in key cities across the UK. It offers modern European cuisine in elegant, yet informal surroundings.

As standard across City Cafe, the restaurants have been designed with floor-to-ceiling windows and outside spaces that can be enjoyed throughout the summer. Mint Hotel Manchester is no exception, with a spacious terrace to soak up the alfresco experience and indulge in a little people-watching in this most cosmopolitan of city centres.

Menus have been thoughtfully designed by Executive Chef Scott Macdonald and these include both classic and contemporary favourites. Locally sourced ingredients are at the heart of every seasonal menu development; combing quality driven dishes, prepared by a skillful team of chefs, at great value.

of award-winning chefs
and carefully prepare the
locally sourced, quality
s to give their customers
est of what is in season

DUCK BALLOTINE WITH RHUBARB CHUTNEY

SERVES 6

🍷 *Katnook Founders Block Coonawarra Cabernet Sauvignon, Australia 2007*

Ingredients

Gingerbread

230g self raising flour
5g bicarbonate of soda
5g ginger (ground)
5g mixed spice
110g butter
110g soft dark brown sugar
110g golden syrup
125g treacle
280ml milk
2 eggs

Rhubarb Chutney

250g of Yorkshire rhubarb
15g shallot (finely chopped)
35g sugar
20ml white wine vinegar
½ star anise
1 cardamom (cracked and shell discarded)

Duck Ballotine

1 duck breast (cooked medium and sliced lengthways)
2 duck legs (confit and shredded)

Two packets of offal to include:

2 gizzards (pan fried and cut in to batons)
2 duck liver (pan fried pink)
1 heart (trimmed and opened pan fried pink)
(If you buy a good quality whole duck from your butcher, or even a supermarket, the livers etc will be inside the bird. If not you can buy the offal separately)
25g pistachios (soaked in boiling water for two hours)
12g chives (finely chopped)
12g chervil (finely chopped)
20g flat parley (finely chopped)
25g warm duck fat
20ml warm jus

Method

For the gingerbread

Boil milk, treacle, golden syrup and spices, then leave to cool. Cream the butter and sugar and slowly add the eggs. Then add the dry ingredients and add the milk mixture afterwards. Bake in a loaf tin for 50 minutes on 150°C.

For the rhubarb chutney

Dice the rhubarb into ½ cm chunks and mix with the sugar. Then place into a bowl and leave it for two hours, straining through a fine sieve and keeping the liquor after this time. In a pan, sweat the chopped shallot without it colouring and add the spices. Add the liquor from the rhubarb and reduce by 2/3rds. Add the rhubarb and half cook it. Remove from the pan and leave to cool; trying to retain as much colour as possible.

For the duck ballotine

Mix all of the ingredients except the herbs and season them. Roll into a 2 inch cylinder using clingfilm and set in the fridge overnight, then remove the film and roll into the herbs. Finally, wrap once again in clingfilm and slice into 3 x 1cm slices.

To serve

Place the 3 slices of ballotine to the right of the plate and a tablespoon of rhubarb chutney to the left. Place the three triangles of gingerbread on a separate plate and serve.

GIGHA HALIBUT WITH FRESH CRAB AND JERSEY ROYALS

SERVES 6

🍷 *A20 Albarino Rias-Baixas,
Spain 2008*

Ingredients

4-6 x 6oz (170g) Gigha halibut portions
150g Jersey Royal potatoes (cooked)
35g shallots (finely diced)
30ml fresh lemon juice
65g pancetta (½cm dice)
65g chorizo (½cm dice)
150g fresh English peas (blanched and shelled)
125g picked white crab meat
12g picked flat parsley
325g pea puree
100ml full fat milk
1 punnet pea cress
salt and pepper

Pea Puree

65g white leek (finely chopped)
3 rashers smoked bacon (finely chopped)
150ml fish stock
150g good quality frozen peas

Method

For the pea puree

Sweat the leek and bacon until soft, then add the fish stock and bring to a rapid boil. Add the peas and boil for 1½ minutes, then remove from the heat and blitz until smooth. Pass through a fine sieve then chill over ice immediately to retain its colour.

For the warm potato salad

Saute the chorizo and pancetta and when crisp add the shallots. Cut the jersey royals into quarters and toss with the pancetta and chorizo. Remove the pan from the heat and add the crab, parsley and lemon juice. Season with a little salt and pepper.

To serve

Pan-fry the halibut and warm the pea puree. Place a circle of pea puree in the centre of a bowl, leaving a little pea puree behind in the pan. Pile the warm potato salad on top of this and place the halibut on top of the potatoes. Froth the milk and fold through the remaining pea puree, then place a line of this across the fish. Finish with a few sprigs of pea cress.

CHOCOLATE BROWNIE, WHITE CHOCOLATE ICE-CREAM

SERVES 4-6

 Maury Grenat, France 2006

Ingredients

Brownie

150g dark chocolate
80g butter
2 small whole eggs
80g sugar
45g flour
55g hazelnuts (roasted)

Creme Pattisier

250ml whole milk
75g sugar
2 egg yolks
25g flour

Chocolate Mousse

175g creme pattisier
175g dark chocolate
250ml double cream (whipped to ribbon stage)

White Chocolate Ice Cream

(this will make 1½ litre tub, keep in the freezer and enjoy any time)
500ml milk
500ml cream
12 egg yolks
250g sugar
320g white chocolate

Chocolate Glaze

150ml water
150g sugar
125ml cream
65g cocoa
40g dark chocolate
2 leaves of gelatine

Method

For the brownie

Melt the chocolate and butter and separately mix the hazelnuts with the flour. Then mix the eggs with the sugar. Fold the nuts and flour with the chocolate and butter, and then add the egg and sugar mix. Fold carefully but thoroughly. Pour the mix into a lined baking tray and bake at 160°C for 35 minutes then allow to cool.

For the creme pattisier

Beat the flour into the egg yolks, then boil the milk and sugar and pour them over the egg yolks. Return to the heat and bring to the boil, whisking all the time. Remove from the heat and allow to cool.

For the chocolate mousse

Melt the chocolate, whisk this into the crème pattisier and fold in the whipped cream.

For the white chocolate ice cream

Put the milk and cream into a pan, add the white chocolate and simmer until the chocolate has melted. Whisk the yolks and sugar until light and fluffy. Bring the white chocolate mix to the boil and whisk the sabayon in. Take off the heat and pass through a fine chinois. Cool and churn in an ice-cream maker. If you are not confident to make ice-cream or don't have time, there are some good quality ice-creams you can buy at your local quality supermarket.

For the chocolate glaze

Bring all of the ingredients apart from the gelatine to the boil. Upon reaching boiling point, add the soaked gelatine and mix through until melted. Pass through a cloth. This can be used straight away.

For the chocolate crisps

Bring the fondant, glucose and isomalt to a 160°C boil, then remove from the heat. Fold in the chocolate and leave to cool. This should then be able to be pulled into long wisps when it is cool. This can be reheated as many times as you wish.

To serve

When the brownie has cooled, top it with an even layer of the mousse approx. ¾ inch thick. Then add the glaze. Cut the brownie into even 3½ inch by 1½ inch rectangles. Brush a little chocolate sauce on the plate with the brownie at the top of the plate, then add a quenelle of the white chocolate ice-cream.

Top the brownie with the chocolate crisps.

THE ELEPHANT AND CASTLE

608 Bury Road, Bamford, Rochdale OL11 4AU

01706 642 277
www.theelephantandcastle.co.uk

Chris Yates is breaking the mould for eating out. His hybrid pub-restaurant - the traditional Elephant and Castle in the Rochdale suburb of Bamford - creates a new 'casual fine dining' category for gourmet tastes.

Chris has worked in some of the North West's best kitchens and with some of its top chefs. From his apprenticeship under Rochdale's resident celebrity chef, Andrew Nutter, he worked under chef-patron Andrew Robinshaw at the legendary award-winning 'Dining Room' in Rawtenstall when it won a two knife-and-fork Michelin Guide rating and was named Restaurant of the Year in the prestigious Hardens Guide.

He was headhunted for 'Dine' in Bolton, was chef de partie at Paul Heathcote's Longridge restaurant, head chef at the Chetham Arms in Chapeltown, and started to attract good reviews as an upcoming young chef at the prestigious White Horse brasserie/bistro at Helmshore.

After becoming a finalist in the 2009 Gordon Ramsay Scholarship, Chris turned down an opportunity to be chef de partie at Ramsay's 3 Michelin Star London restaurant in order to turn his Lancashire pub, the Shoulder of Mutton, into a profitable food-led business that won Newcomer of the Year in the Great British Pub Awards.

Now he has added the Elephant and Castle, which promises to overturn all remaining preconceptions about conventional pub-restaurants.

timothypaulbradley 2

Chris Yates at the Elephant and Castle in Bamford, Rochdale, is breaking the mould as a hybrid pub-restaurant that creates a new 'casual fine dining' category for gourmet tastes.

PAN ROASTED HAND DIVED SCALLOPS, GLAZED PORK BELLY, JASMINE PICKLED MOOLI AND APRICOT

SERVES 5

*Finca La Chamiza, Polo Amateur Chardonnay
Mendoza, Argentina*

Method

For the pork belly

Place the pork belly in a deep, large tray and season. Pour over the apple cider and cook at 70°C for 8 hours. Once cooked, remove and leave to chill in the fridge.

For the mooli

Peel the Mooli lengthways, then peel it into ribbons. Place the dried jasmine tea leaves, honey and water into a saucepan and bring them to the boil. Add the Mooli to the liquor for 30 seconds then remove and chill.

For the apricots

Dice the Apricots and pan-fry them with the sugar until golden brown and sticky, almost like a chutney. Remove and chill.

To finish

Heat a frying pan with a little oil then season the scallops and pan fry for 30 seconds on each side. Slice the pork belly into 1cm thick slices and add to the pan again for another 30 seconds on each side.

To serve

Remove both from the pan and assemble as in the picture. Garnish the dish as you please with salad cress.

Ingredients

5 large, hand dived scallops
½ pork belly
2 bottles apple cider (approx 500ml)
50g Jasmine tea leaves (dried)
1 mooli
6 apricots
2 tbsp honey
75ml water
50g caster sugar
25ml olive oil

WEST PENNINE SPRING LAMB THREE WAYS, ROASTED BEST END, SWEETBREAD AND KIDNEY. ASPARAGUS MOUSSE, HOT-POT PRESSING

SERVES 5

🍷 Zonin Ripasso Della Valpolicella,
Italy

Ingredients

5 x 400g best end french trimmed lamb (ask your butcher to do this)
3 x 160g lamb sweetbreads
2 bunches of asparagus
3 large Maris Pipers
2 swedes
5 carrots
1 onion
500ml brown chicken sock
500ml beef stock
50ml red wine
2 gelatine leaves
6 tbsp water
200ml double cream
3 egg whites
50g salt

Method

For the hot-pot pressing

Peel the potatoes, swedes and carrots and thinly slice on a Japanese mandolin.

Thinly slice the onion then slowly sauté in a little oil until it goes translucent.

Layer the vegetables with the onions and season each layer with salt. Add layers into a deep casserole pot and cover with the chicken stock. Cover the pot in tin foil and cook at 120°C for 1 hour 45 minutes.

For the asparagus mousse

Cook the asparagus in boiling water until tender (approx 3 minutes), then cool in ice water and put through a food processor to obtain a smooth puree. Cover the gelatine leaves with water and soak them until they become soft. Whisk the egg whites until stiff and fold into the asparagus mousse, then add the cream and the soft gelatine and allow them to set in a fridge for 3 hours.

Finally, cut the asparagus mousse into 3cm diced cubes.

For the lamb and sweetbread

Blanch and peel the membrane from the sweetbread, then set aside.

Add a little oil to a hot frying pan, brown the lamb on all sides, then remove and allow to rest for 5 minutes. Repeat with the sweetbreads.

Add the red wine to the hot frying pan and reduce by half. Then add the beef stock and reduce by half again. This is the sauce for the dish.

To serve

Assemble the dish as in the picture with a selection of vegetables of your choice.

ASSIETTE OF APPLE, APPLE DOUGHNUTS, APPLE AND LEMON CANNELLONI, APPLE BARVOIS

SERVES 5

 Chateau Manos,
Cadillac Bordeaux

Ingredients

Apple Leather

7 Granny Smith apples (peeled and chopped)
300ml water
300g sugar
1 vanilla pod
1 lemon

Lemon Curd

75g caster sugar
1 lemon (zest and juice)
2 eggs
50g butter

Doughnuts

225g strong plain flour
2g salt
8g fresh yeast
20g caster sugar
100ml milk
10g butter (melted)
1 egg

Apple Barvois

100g egg whites
200ml apple juice
6 Granny Smith apples (peeled and diced)
4 leaves gelatine
150ml double cream
6 egg yolks
200g caster sugar

Method

For the apple leather

Place apples, sugar, water and half the lemon into a pan and bring to a steady simmer for 5-10 minutes. When soft, blend in a food processor and pass through a sieve.

Place 1 half of the apple puree into a container and refrigerate. Spread the other half onto a greaseproof paper-lined tray to 2mm deep. Place in a warm area of the kitchen to dry naturally, until it becomes stretchable.

For the lemon curd

Whisk together the sugar and eggs in a bowl over a pan of simmering water until it reaches the ribbon stage. Add the lemon juice and zest, and then add the diced butter slowly until the mix thickens. Allow to cool.

For the doughnuts

Warm the milk with the butter, then add sugar and yeast. In a food processor, add the remaining dry ingredients and the egg to form a dough.

Mix the dough for 10 minutes and, once elastic, move the mixture onto a floured surface. Cut the dough into 25g balls.

Place the doughnuts onto a lightly oiled baking tray. Heat a deep fat fryer to 180°C then carefully drop the doughnut into the fryer, 5 at time, until golden brown.

Fill the doughnuts by piercing a little hole in each doughnut and filling it with the apple mixture.

Portion the apple leather into 10cm x 5cm rectangles, roll into a cylinders and fill with the lemon curd.

For the apple barvois

Boil 2 teaspoons of water with 150g of the sugar to form a syrup. This takes 6 minutes on a high heat. Whisk the egg whites until stiff then slowly pour the syrup into the egg whites while still whisking. Continue whisking for 6 minutes. This is your meringue.

Bring the diced apple, cream and apple juice to the boil. When the apples are soft, puree in a food processor. Then whisk in the egg yolk and fold in the meringue. Place onto a thin baking tray and chill for 20 minutes.

To serve

Assemble the dish as in the picture.

060
EVUNA

227-229 Deansgate, Manchester M3 4EW

0161 819 2752
www.evuna.com

Evuna is a fine Spanish restaurant and wine bar situated right in the heart of Manchester. Our restaurant aims to offer you the finest in Spanish food and drink with food that originates from all regions of Spain, ranging from tapas to a la carte. Our signature dish is Seabass Baked in Rock Salt, which is filleted fabulously at your table, and all our produce is cooked fresh daily on the premises.

At the restaurant we also offer a wine merchant service, where customers can take their favourite wines home with them both by the bottle or by the case. In our small shop area you can browse some of these offers whilst enjoying a glass of wine and some tapas.

We import over 100 different types of Spanish wine from every corner of Spain. Our philosophy is to bring you only the finest wines from family run vineyards that use traditional wine making methods, many of them exclusive to Evuna.

Corporate events are our speciality. We offer formal wine tastings with an experienced host to guide you and your guests through the world of quality Spanish wines, or informal events without a speaker so that you can taste and network at your leisure.

Our tastings are innovative and fun, and pitched at a level that ensures everyone learns something new whatever their wine knowledge. We turn wine education into first-class entertainment so that your guests leave with the confidence to tackle the wine list at the next company dinner!

Our restaurant aims to offer you the finest in Spanish food and drink with food that originates from all regions of Spain, ranging from tapas to a la carte

BACALAO CROQUETTES

SERVES 6-8

Trascampanas 2010,
Rueda, Verdejo

Ingredients

Croquettes

500g salt cod
1 lemon rind (grated)
2 tbsp nutmeg
salt and pepper
100g chives
500g potatoes (boiled and mashed)
½ white onion (diced)
200g parsley
2 egg yolks
200g breadcrumbs
vegetable oil

Alioli
6 egg yolks
1 clove garlic (finely chopped)
250ml extra virgin oil
juice from 1 lemon

Garnish
lemon wedges

Method

For the cod

You will need to start this recipe one day in advance.

Place the cod in a bowl and cover with water. Place in the fridge for 24 hours, changing the water from time to time (3-4 times).

Bring 1 litre of water to the boil in a pan for 10 minutes. Add the cod, onion, lemon rind and nutmeg and cook for 5 minutes. Drain the salt cod and allow to cool. Add mashed potatoes, 1 egg yolk and 50g of the breadcrumbs and mix together.

Season with salt and pepper, add the chives and stir to combine. Remove from heat and transfer to a container. Allow to cool then place in the fridge for 2 hours or until set.

Divide the cod mixture into approximately 18 portions (about the length of a hand and width of half a hand). Dust in flour, shaking away any excess. Dip the croquettes, one at a time, in egg then evenly coat in breadcrumbs. Place croquettes on a tray, cover, and place in the fridge for 1 hour to set.

For the alioli

Place the egg yolks and garlic in a food processor and mix until combined. With the motor running, gradually add the oil in a thin, steady stream until mixture is thick. Then add the lemon juice, salt and pepper and process until smooth.

To assemble

Heat enough vegetable oil in a deep frying pan to reach a depth of 7cm and place over a high heat. Add half the croquettes and cook, turning occasionally, for 2 minutes or until golden brown. Use a slotted spoon to transfer to a plate lined with paper towels to absorb any excess oil. Repeat with the remaining croquettes.

To serve

Serve immediately with lemon wedges and alioli.

Chef's tip

The vegetable oil is ready when a cube of bread turns golden in 15 seconds.

SEAFOOD PAELLA

SERVES 1

Finca de Arantei 2009,
Rias baixas, Albarino

Ingredients

130g rice
100g of mixed chop vegetables (pepper, onion,
carrots, parsley)
1 clove garlic
1½ tbsp paprika
200ml fish stock
200ml water
100g calamares
100g hake (chopped)
100g small prawns
4 king prawns
50g fresh mussels
extra virgin olive oil
pinch of saffron

Method

Pour 2 tablespoons of extra virgin olive into a paella pan. Once the oil is hot add the onion then fry for 1 minute, followed by the rest of vegetables. Add paprika and fry all together for 1 minute.

Add the squid, hake and prawns and fry for another minute, then add garlic and fry for a further minute.

Add water and fish stock infused with saffron and bring to the boil.

Add rice then lower the heat. Cover with tinfoil and cook for 20 minutes, adding the mussels at the 17 minute mark to steam.

Season to taste.

To serve

Assemble as in the picture.

SPANISH CHEESECAKE

SERVES 16

 Senorio de sarria,
Navarra, Moscatel

Method

Beat the egg yolks and egg whites with the sugar, lemon zest and vanilla essence until a pale yellow colour, then add the remaining ingredients (mascarpone, Philadelphia) and stir together until the mixture in evenly incorporated.

Ladle the cheese filling into a non-stick tin.

Place the tin onto bain-marie and cook for 1 hour and 30 minutes at 160°C.

To serve

Cut a slice of cheesecake and serve with a sliced strawberry, one scoop of the finest vanilla ice cream and a drizzle of raspberry syrup, or simply serve alone.

Ingredients

10 egg yolks
6 egg white
440ml double cream
420g Philadelphia cheese
320g mascarpone
330g sugar
lemon zest
2 tsp vanilla essence

Garnish

scoop of good quality vanilla ice cream
raspberry sauce (optional)
1 strawberry (sliced)

070
JEM & I

1C School Lane, Didsbury, Manchester M20 6RD

0161 445 3996
www.jemandirestaurant.co.uk

The Michelin recommended Jem & I Restaurant continues to thrive as Didsbury's most acclaimed restaurant, picking up awards for Best Restaurant (Cheshire Life 2008-09) and the proprietor and head chef, Jem O'Sullivan, winning Best Chef (Manchester Food and Dink Festival 1999). Sitting at the heart of Didsbury village Jem & I Restaurant provides consistent quality and a modern dining experience, day in and day out, to our ever increasing customer base.

The vibrant and fast paced lunch service boasts a comprehensive a la carte menu as well as a constantly changing Express Lunch menu for those looking for a quality, quick bite to eat for £5. Perfect for those ladies wanting to catch up with friends, business colleagues on a lunch meeting, or staff from the local schools on their lunch break.

The evening service offers a more leisurely paced dining experience, with an ever evolving a la carte menu and extensive wine list. An early diners menu runs along side our a la carte menu until 7pm. We have a daily specials board boasting a starter, fish and meat dish. We also try out dishes to gage popularity for potential changes to the menu. Diners come from all areas to sample our Modern European style cuisine, from the local village to the heart of Cheshire and beyond. We host anything from couples wanting a quiet intimate dinner, right through to large birthday celebrations or business meals.

Sitting at the heart of Didsbury village, Jem & I Restaurant provides consistent quality and a modern dining experience, day in and day out, to our ever increasing customer base

SEARED HAND DIVED SCALLOPS WITH CAULIFLOWER PUREE, SPICED CAULIFLOWER FRITTERS AND WATERCRESS SALAD

SERVES 4

Gruner Veltliner, Stadlmann, Austria 2008

Ingredients

12 large scallops
splash of olive oil

Cauliflower Puree

½ large cauliflower
2 banana shallots
1 clove garlic
50g butter
dash of cream

Fritters

½ large cauliflower
1 bottle of lager
plain flour
1 tsp curry powder

Garnish

1 bunch of watercress
50ml olive oil
1 lemon

Method

For the fritters

Floret the cauliflower and set aside ½ for the puree. Blanch it in boiling, salted water until al dente, then refresh in iced water. Make a batter with the lager and plain flour and add the curry powder and a little salt. Just before serving, dip the florets in the batter and fry until hot and crisp.

For the puree

Slice the shallots and the rest of the cauliflower. Add 30g butter and the garlic to a saucepan on a medium heat and cook until soft. Blend into a puree - if needed add a dash of cream - and season to taste.

For the scallops

Heat a sautee pan and add a splash of olive oil, then sear the scallops on one side until golden, turn, and add the rest of the butter. Then set aside.

To serve

Place a quarter of the puree in the centre of a plate and alternate between one scallop and one fritter around the puree. Place a good sprig of watercress on the puree. Mix some lemon and olive oil, and use it to dress the watercress and drizzle around the plate.

ROAST RACK AND LOIN OF LAMB WITH BUTTERNUT SQUASH GRATIN, CONFIT LEEKS, FRENCH BEANS, ROSTI POTATO, ROAST GARLIC AND ROSEMARY JUS

SERVES 4

Dreambay Pinot Noir 2008, Marlborough, New Zealand

Ingredients

500g 8 bone rack of lamb
300g loin or saddle of lamb

Gratin

1 large butternut squash
2 cloves of garlic
8 sage leaves (chopped)
200g butter (diced into cubes)
dash of cream
50g grated parmesan

Rosti

4 Maris Piper potatoes
vegetable oil

Vegetables

1 medium leek
200g french beans
25g butter

Jus

2 pints of lamb or beef stock
rosemary
250ml red wine

Method

For the lamb

Start by seasoning the lamb. Then heat a frying pan and seal the rack and saddle before placing it in a hot oven (220°C) for 8-12 minutes, depending on your preference. Set it aside to rest before carving. A good portion is to carve 2 racks and 3 slices of loin per person.

For the gratin

Peel and dice the squash and place it in a deep roasting tray with the sage, whole garlic, butter and roast at 200°C until soft. Then mash them together. Place in small ramekins and top with cream and parmesan, then return them to the oven and bake for 8 minutes or until top is nicely baked.

For the rosti potato

Grate the potatoes then put some of the grated potato and a little oil into 4 inch rings. Heat a frying pan until smoking and cook them until crisp on one side, then turn until crisp on both sides.

For the vegetables

Trim the French beans and blanch in a pan of boiling, salted water. Then refresh in cold water. Slice the leek and sweat in a frying pan on a medium heat with a little butter. When soft, add the cooked beans and warm through.

For the jus

Reduce the red wine in a saucepan until virtually evaporated then add the stock and rosemary. Reduce again by three quarters. Finish with a small knob of butter, just before serving. Season to taste.

To serve

Assemble as in picture with roast whole cloves of garlic and a sprig of rosemary to garnish.

CREME BRULEE TART WITH BLUEBERRY COMPOTE

SERVES 6-8

Hollick 'The Nectar', Coonawarra, Australia

Ingredients

Pastry

8 inch tart case
250g plain flour
125g butter (diced)
50g caster sugar
1 egg

Filling

12 egg yolks
170g caster sugar
1 litre double cream
½ vanilla pod (split)

Blueberry Compote

500g blueberries
100g caster sugar

Method

For the pastry

Rub the butter into the flour, then add the sugar and bind with the egg. Leave to rest before rolling out to the thickness of a £1 coin. Then line the tart case and blind bake.

For the filling

Warm the cream and vanilla pod. Mix yolks and sugar (but do not over mix). Gradually add the cream, gently stirring, and then allow it to cool. Add the mix to the pastry case and bake on 160°C for 25-30 minutes until set. Leave to cool, then place in fridge until cold.

For the compote

Put 250g of the blueberries in a saucepan with the caster sugar and heat until fallen, then add the rest of the blueberries and heat until just softened.

To serve

Slice the tart, top with caster sugar and brulee with blow torch. Garnish with compote and cream.

080
JODRELL BANK

The Planet Pavillion Cafe, Jodrell Bank Discovery Centre, University of Manchester, Macclesfield SK11 9DW

01477 571 321
www.themoderncaterer.co.uk

Jodrell bank is the latest venue from The Modern Caterer, home to the world famous Lovell Telescope, set in the heart of rural Cheshire.

Peter Booth aka The Modern Caterer has been cooking his simple, fresh, seasonal food for Mancunians and the international community alike for nearly 10 years now, at nowhere more noteably than the Whitworth Art Gallery.

The majestic settings of the Whitworth Art Gallery provided the perfect backdrop for The Modern Caterer to firmly establish itself on the gastromic map of the North West. With a steady stream of prestigious awards and new openings, followed by the critically acclaimed Gabriel's Kitchen and Chorlton's new casual eatery Gabriel's Grocery Store.

Booth was born in Liverpool and travelled from an early age to London, Europe, the Americas and the Middle East, exploring local foods and culture along the way.

Expect expertly sourced produce, fresh, punchy world flavours and classic British comfort food at all venues.

The Whitworth Art Gallery, winner of The Good Food Guide Best Family Restaurant 2009

BRUSCHETTA OF VINE TOMATOES, BUFFALO MOZZARELLA & BASIL

SERVES 4

Fairhills Fairtrade Mendoza Chardonnay

Method

For the tomatoes

Wash the tomatoes, take out the core and roughly dice. Shred the basil leaves and add to tomatoes. Add three tablespoons of oil and season to taste. Set aside.

For the bruschetta

Toast the sour dough bread on both sides, ideally on a griddle. Cut the garlic clove in half and rub across the one side of each piece of the bruschetta bread. Slightly flatten all the bruschetta, pushing down on each one with the palm of your hand. Divide three tablespoons of oil between the four pieces, allowing the bread to soak up the oil "rather like lashings of butter".

To serve

Place the bruschetta onto the centre of each plate. Divide the tomato and basil mixture between the four bruschetta, allowing it to fall off naturally. Tear each ball of mozzarella into two pieces and place on top quite rustically.

Add a twist of pepper from the mill to the top of each dish and add a nice plush of basil for garnish. Finally drizzle with the remaining oil around the plate and serve.

Ingredients

2 balls of finest Buffalo mozzarella
1 kg of finest British vine tomatoes
small bunch basil (approx 50g)
fine sea salt
freshly ground black pepper
9 tbsp extra virgin olive oil
1 clove garlic
4 thick slices artisan sour dough bread

PAPPARDELLE PASTA, NEW SEASON COURGETTES, PEAS, PECORINO CHEESE & TOASTED ALMONDS

SERVES 4

 Fairhills Fairtrade Mendoza
Chardonnay

Gabriel's Grocery

Ingredients

500g de cecco pappardelle pasta
2 small courgettes (finely sliced)
200g best quality frozen peas (this is the only
frozen product we would recommend) defrosted
½ clove garlic (finely chopped)
large knob of butter
zest of half a lemon
20g toasted almonds
50g bunch of flat leaf parsley (finely shredded)
40g pecorino cheese
fine sea salt
freshly ground black pepper
4 tbsp of extra virgin olive oil

Method

For the pasta

Fill a large saucepan with water, bring it to a rolling boil and season with salt (It should taste of the sea). Add the pasta and cook for approx six or seven minutes until al dente.

Whilst the pasta is cooking, heat a large frying pan on a low heat and add the butter and olive oil. Add the courgettes and fry until lightly coloured, season to taste. Add the garlic and gently fry. Do not allow to colour. Add the peas and season again slightly.

Strain the pasta, reserving some of the cooking liquor. Add the pasta to the frying pan along with the parsley and the lemon zest. Toss thoroughly and check the seasoning. Add a little of the cooking liquor to create a little steam and add moisture.

To serve

Using tongues, divide evenly between the plates, trying your best to create some height. Grate the pecorino generously onto each dish. Divide the toasted almonds, drizzle a little oil and serve.

Bon Appetit!

FAIR TRADE CHOCOLATE AND WALNUT BROWNIES, VANILLA ICE CREAM

SERVES 20

Handmade Elderflower Sparkle by Lovely

Ingredients

Brownie

375g unsalted butter
375g fair-trade dark chocolate
6 free range eggs
1 tbsp vanilla extract
500g caster sugar
225g plain flour
1 tsp salt
300g walnuts (chopped)
baking tin measuring
(approx 30cm x 25cm x 6cm)

Ice Cream

2 vanilla pods
500ml double cream
70g caster sugar
3 free range egg yolks

Method

Preheat the oven to 180°C and line the tin with baking parchment.

Melt the butter and chocolate together in a heavy based pan over a low heat.

Whisk the eggs with the sugar and vanilla in a mixing bowl.

Allow the chocolate mixture to cool a little then whisk it into the eggs and sugar mix.

Sieve the flour into the mixture and add the nuts. Mix well.

Bake for 25 minutes or until it is set with a slight wobble in the middle. Allow to cool and refrigerate for 20 minutes before cutting.

For the ice cream

No ice cream churner required!

Halve the vanilla pods length ways and scrape out the seeds. Add the pods to the cream and bring to the boil, then add the sugar and stir until the sugar has dissolved.

Meanwhile, whisk the egg yolks in a large bowl then slowly whisk in the hot cream mixture.

Pour the mixture through a fine sieve into another bowl and whisk in the vanilla seeds. Pour the mixture into a freezer-proof container and freeze for 2-3 hours, or until set.

To serve

Portion the brownies as you wish and serve with a scoop of home-made ice cream.

Chef's tip

Seasonal English strawberries go well and look great as a garnish.

090
MALMAISON MANCHESTER

Piccadilly, Manchester M1 1LZ

0161 278 1000
www.malmaison.com

No "Smoak" without Malmaison in Manchester.

A grill room and bar quite unlike anything Manchester has ever seen before and set in the award winning Malmaison Hotel, minutes from Piccadilly station, Smoak is total indulgence for the senses. The amazing aroma of a nation's finest char-grilled steaks and fresh fish, served to a pewter counter or a cosy booth. Imagine great imported beers, cocktails and bubbly served from an unusual sunken bar, with highly skilled mixologists serving you while you stay seated. Picture a stylish, relaxed but chic interior; a mix of booths, banquettes and counter stools. Come lunchtime, and its locally sourced bread, generously filled sandwiches and salads, or full blown grill dining for the more adventurous lunchtime escapee. Come sundown, the mood changes and we turn the aromas up to eleven. The cocktails flow, the steaks sizzle, the music turns up and the night begins.

We could tell you about the Ember Lounge - an immaculate and opulent cocktail bar, furtively hidden to the rear of the bar. But your name's not on the list, so you can't come in.

Smoak Bar and Grill - That's Malmaison. Different again.

A grill room and bar quite unlike anything Manchester has ever seen before and set in the award-winning Malmaison Hotel, minutes from Piccadilly station

SEA BREAM WITH RICOTTA AND SPRING ONION RAVIOLI, CHIVE SAUCE

SERVES 4

🍷 *Pinot Grigio Dolomiti Alois Lageder, Italy*

Ingredients

Sea Bream

2 fillets of sea bream
100g samphire
salt and pepper

Ricotta Ravioli

300g flour
6 egg yolks
1 beaten egg
extra virgin olive oil
80g ricotta
2 spring onions

Chive Sauce

1 shallot
60ml dry white wine
100ml double cream
fresh chives
40g butter

Method

For the ricotta ravioli

Combine the flour with the egg yolks in a food processor. Then splash a little virgin olive oil and blend until it's smooth and not sticky. Wrap the dough in clingfilm and keep to rest in the fridge for at least 1 hour. Prepare the pasta filling by mixing the ricotta with finely chopped spring onions, and season with salt and pepper.

Roll the pasta dough with a pasta roller or rolling pin until it is about 2mm thick and cut the dough into circles with a 6cm cutter. Brush half of these with beaten egg and place about a tablespoon full of filling on each. Then use another pasta ring to seal them.

Cook the ravioli in salted water until al dente. When cooked, toss in a pan with little bit of butter.

For the chive sauce

Dice the peeled shallot and sweat with a little butter, then add white wine and reduce by about half.

Pass this through a fine sieve, add double cream, season and reduce by a further half. Then add diced chives, and a knob of soft butter and blitz with hand blender until light and foamy.

For the fish

Bone and trim the bream fillets then cut into 4 pieces.

Fry skin-side down for about 3 minutes until crispy, then turn and quickly finish the other side.

Melt the butter in the frying pan and quickly fry the samphire for about a minute to keep it crispy.

To serve

Assemble as seen in the picture.

FILLET OF PORK WRAPPED IN PANCETTA WITH BOULANGERE POTATOES, ARMAGNAC PRUNES AND CIDER FOAM

SERVES 4

*Spy Valley Pinot Noir,
New Zealand*

Ingredients

Boulangere Potatoes

1 onion
750g Maris Piper potatoes
225ml vegetable or chicken stock
1 tbsp olive oil
fresh thyme

Cider Foam

1 bramley apple
2 shallots
200ml cider
200ml double cream
100ml thick veal stock

Pork Wrapped in Pancetta

4 x 180g pork fillet steaks
16 thin slices of pancetta
12 dry prunes
50ml Armagnac (or brandy)

Method

Soak the prunes in armagnac overnight.

For the boulangere potatoes

Thinly slice the onion and fry for few minutes until soft and lightly coloured. Next, thinly slice the peeled potatoes then oil the sides of a gratin dish and start layering the potatoes and onions. After each layer, sprinkle with some of the thyme leaves. Make sure that the top layer will be potatoes, then pour on the stock and place in an oven heated to about 180°C and bake for about 1 hour until soft and golden on top.

For the cider foam

Dice the shallots and peeled apple and fry them in a saucepan until the apple is caramelised and golden, then add cider and reduce until almost dry. Pour in double cream and reduce by half then add the veal stock. Blend with a hand blender, season, and pass through a fine sieve.

When ready to serve, pour the cider sauce into a cream whipper to turn it into foam.

For the pork

Season your pork fillets and wrap each portion in 4 slices of pancetta. Pan-fry until the pancetta is golden and crispy, then place in the oven at 200°C and bake for about 8 minutes, then allow to rest.

To serve

Slice a portion of boulangere potatoes and heat up the prunes with a little knob of butter. Cut the pork fillet into a few slices and assemble as in the picture.

CARAMEL AND RASPBERRY PANNA COTTA

SERVES 4

🍷 *Sauternes*
French Dessert Wine

Ingredients

Panna Cotta

150g caster sugar
2 tbsp of liquid glucose
300ml double cream
80ml milk
1½ gelatine leaves
1 tbsp of rum

Tuile Crisp

125g butter (melted)
150g icing sugar
100g egg white
125g plain flour
20g freeze dried raspberries (smashed into powder)

Method

For the panna cotta

Firstly make the caramel. Put half of the sugar in a heavy based saucepan with the glucose and 30ml of water. Put the liquid on a low heat and stir occasionally until it no longer feels gritty. Then raise the heat and let the syrup bubble until it attains a nice caramel colour. When the caramel is ready, quickly take the pan off the heat and cool the caramel by placing the pan in a water basin with iced water. Keep it there for about 2 minutes to stop it from burning.

Now put the milk and cream into the saucepan and slowly bring to the boil. Keep boiling for about 5 minutes to reduce the mixture. Meanwhile, put the gelatine into a bowl of cold water to soak. When the liquid is reduced, add the remaining sugar and rum and allow it to dissolve, then remove from the heat and cool for 2 minutes. Put in the softened gelatine and stir until it dissolves, then leave on the side to cool down.

Take 4 moulds (about 100ml capacity) and spoon about 2 spoons of warm caramel into each of them, then slowly pour the mix into them, filling the moulds right to the top. Now chill until set, preferably overnight.

For the tuile crisp

Mix butter, sugar, egg whites and flour together into a smooth paste and leave to rest in the fridge for a few hours. Then thinly spread onto a tray with baking paper into the desired shapes. Finally, sprinkle with some of the dry powdered raspberries and bake in an oven on 150°C until golden and crispy.

To serve

Assemble as in the picture.

100
THE MARK ADDY

Stanley Street, Salford, Manchester M3 5EJ

0161 832 4080
www.markaddy.co.uk

I n an Observer review, Executive Head Chef of The Mark Addy, Robert Owen Brown, was described as having a touch of the Dickens character about him; one of those sturdy, reliable types who turn up for a few chapters when everything is looking bleak for the hero and hangs about the page, looking like a place of safety. He has ginger curls, wears unbuttoned waistcoats, calls men sir and women madam in a way that is unforced and has a robust response to anything he considers pretentious.

The Mark Addy is located on the Salford side of the River Irwell, opposite the People's History Museum and approximately 200 yards from Manchester's main thoroughfare, Deansgate. Despite being in Salford, it has a reputation for excellence that could belong to an establishment in any city in the world, and it is regarded as one of Manchester's leading restaurants in this Tale of Two Cities!

Rob's passion is for locally-sourced, English food, and he is steadfast in pursuit of provenance, quality and originality. His Specials list changes daily and can include anything from tripe, faggots and hogget, to leagram's day old curd cheese. In the pursuit of fresh produce and quality presentation a crown of pigeon, shot in the hills outside the city, can end up being presented with a shotgun cartridge on the plate.

The menu is extensive, catering to those looking for renowned food in portions ranging from a quick nibble to a single course to a fine lunch or hearty dinner, with something to suit all tastes including vegetarian options. "The Chef's Menu" especially is a real treat, though usually this must be pre-ordered. We could rename it Great Expectations!

The Mark Addy is named after a local boatman who reputedly saved a total of 51 people from drowning in the Irwell, for which he received the Albert Medal, later called the Victoria Cross. Coincidentally he died on 9th June 1890, twenty years to the day after Charles Dickens.

Robert Owen Brown's passion is for locally-sourced, English food, and he is steadfast in pursuit of provenance, quality and originality

BLACK PUDDING POTATO CAKE WITH SOFT POACHED EGG AND TANGY TARRAGON SAUCE

SERVES 4

Paarl Heights Chenin Blanc, South Africa

Method

For the potato cake

Mix together the potato, parsley, chopped chives, black pudding and a little seasoning and form them into a hockey puck shape.

Crack 2 eggs into a bowl and beat them. Then coat your potato cakes, first in flour, then in the egg, and finally in breadcrumbs. Then place on a tray in the fridge.

For tarragon sauce

In a heavy-bottomed pan, reduce the cream by half and add 5ml of white wine vinegar and seasoning to taste. Add the tarragon and leave to stand.

To finish

Pre-heat your deep fat fryer to 180°C and your oven to 200°C. Deep fry the potato cakes until they are golden, then place on a baking tray in the oven for 7 minutes.

Next, boil water in a pan, adding the remaining vinegar, and then turn down to a simmer before dropping in the eggs. By the time the eggs are poached your potato cakes should be ready.

To serve

Top each cake with a soft poached egg, drizzle with the tarragon sauce and dress with the uncut chives.

Ingredients

Potato Cake

170g potato (finely mashed)
170g black pudding (1cm diced)
1 spoon each of parsley and chives (chopped)
6 eggs
170g fine breadcrumbs
55g plain flour
55g unsalted butter
pinch of salt and pepper

Tarragon Sauce

1 spoon tarragon (chopped)
10ml tsp white wine vinegar
140ml cream

Garnish

8 uncut chives to decorate

STUFFED PIG'S TROTTER

SERVES 2

🍷 *Moko Black Pinot Noir, Central Otago, New Zealand 2009/10*

Ingredients

Stuffing

1 onion (chopped)
60g butter
170g fresh white breadcrumbs
30g black pudding (finely chopped)
110g bacon (minced)
5 sprigs of fresh thyme
1 egg (beaten)
salt and pepper

Trotter

4 carrots (halved)
2 onions (chopped)
5 sprigs of fresh thyme
1 pig's trotter (boned)
300ml chicken stock

Potato

450g Maris Piper potatoes
60g butter
pinch of salt and pepper
splash of double cream
small handful of chives (chopped)

Method

Preheat oven to 190°C.

For the stuffing

Pick the leaves from the thyme and chop finely.

Add the butter to a frying pan, heat, add the onion and cook until softened.

Remove from the pan and add the breadcrumbs, bacon, black pudding and thyme.

Season and add the egg, stirring well to bind it together. Use this to stuff the trotter and tie it shut.

For the trotter

In a lidded, oven-proof dish arrange the carrots, onions and thyme, placing the trotter on top.

Pour over the stock and cook for 2 – 3 hours. Cover with the lid if necessary to avoid over- browning the dish.

For the potato

Boil the potatoes first then add the other ingredients and mash.

To serve

Reduce the left over cooking stock in a saucepan over a high heat.

Add the meat to the centre of the plate. Using the piping bag, pipe the chive mash around the trotter and then pour over the reduced stock to finish.

ROBERT OWEN BROWN'S TREACLE TART

SERVES 4

🍷 *Fernando de Castilla - Antique Px*
Jerez Spain

Ingredients

Treacle Tart

500ml cream
500ml golden syrup
100g butter (melted)
250g bread crumbs
4 egg yolks
4 x 3 inch, pre prepared pastry cases

Lemon & Thyme Ice Cream

100g egg yolk
120g sugar
250ml double cream
250ml milk
40g glucose syrup
1 handful thyme leaves
zest and juice of 2 lemons

Method

For the treacle tart

Mix all of the ingredients together and pour them into the 4 pre-prepared pastry cases.

Bake at 180°C for 45 minutes until golden.

For the lemon & thyme ice cream

Whisk the egg yolk and 80g of the sugar until stiff and pale.

Slowly heat the milk, cream and glucose syrup until they begin to boil, then remove from heat.

Stirring constantly, slowly add the hot cream mixture to the sugar and eggs.

Add the picked thyme leaves and whisk over an ice bath until chilled.

Strain the ice cream, mixing to remove the thyme, then stir in the lemon zest

Heat the lemon juice and the remaining 40g of sugar in a pan to make a light syrup, then set aside to cool slightly.

Churn the chilled ice cream mix and, with the machine still running, pour in the lemon syrup.

Freeze for 1 hour before serving.

To serve

Place the treacle tart on to a plate followed by a scoop of ice cream. We like to garnish the dish with a spun sugar cage as in the picture.

110 MARKET RESTAURANT

104 High Street, Manchester M4 1HQ

0161 834 3743
www.market-restaurant.com

Located in Manchester's trendy Northern Quarter, situated between Piccadilly and Ancoats, this was the central trading area of Victorian Manchester; bustling activity from dawn until dusk; a 24 hour economy fostered by the development of Smithfield Market and the continued growth of the cotton industry.

Today a centre of alternative and bohemian culture; the home of fashion designers and art galleries; curry houses and architects; council houses and craft centres; designer hairstylists and market traders; florists and shirt makers; recording studios, renowned music and comedy venues, record labels and creative agencies; a Methodist Hall and a Buddhist Centre; Dickensian pubs and quirky retailers.

The Market Restaurant has been a torchbearer in the Northern Quarter for over 30 years. "When this place opened, the potential of the area had been recognised but few had dared to commit cash. The Market led the way and now sits proudly on the most interesting food and drink street in North West England." – City Life

We place an accent on the quality of our ingredients rather than the length of our menu. All of the preparation and cooking of the food is done here on the premises.

We avoid convenience pre frozen, pre packed and synthetic products and use fresh, wholesome foods, cooking them in ways that lose as little of their nutrients and flavour as is possible. We source most our ingredients from local producers and suppliers. Some guests get it immediately, others unfortunately don't. Our reward is in those guests who recognise the results of our efforts and return again and again.

RESTAUR

At The Market Restaurant, we place an accent on the quality of our ingredients rather than the length of our menu. All of the preparation and cooking of the food is done here on the premises

PARSNIPS MOLLY PARKIN

SERVES 4

*Chablis 1er Cru "Les Vaillons", Domaine Bernard
AC – France*

Ingredients

960g parsnips
480g tomatoes
5 tbsp oil
90g butter
3 tbsp soft brown sugar
salt and black pepper
180g Gruyere cheese (grated)
300ml single or double cream
4 tbsp fresh white breadcrumbs

Method

Peel the parsnips, cut away and discard any hard, central cores and thinly slice them. Then skin the tomatoes and remove the seeds, cutting the flesh into slices.

Heat the oil in a pan and lightly fry the parsnips for 4 minutes.

Grease a casserole dish with half the butter and place a layer of parsnips over the base. Sprinkle these with a little sugar, salt and freshly ground pepper and then add a little cream. Now cover with a layer of tomatoes. Spread a little more cream and then sprinkle the grated cheese over the tomatoes.

Repeat these layers until all the ingredients are used up, finishing off with cream and cheese. Top with the breadcrumbs and dot with the remaining butter.

Cook the parsnip casserole for 40 minutes in the centre of a pre-heated oven at 325 F/160°C or gas mark 3.

To serve

Serve straight from the casserole dish.

VENISON MEDALLIONS WITH BLACKCURRANT SAUCE

SERVES 4

🍷 *Valopolicella Ripassor Sospiro*
Italy

Ingredients

Venison

500g venison medallions
1 tbsp olive oil
60g butter
red wine (for marinating venison overnight)

Blackcurrant Sauce

100ml port
100ml red wine
50ml crème de cassis
1 tsp double cream
black pepper
100g blackcurrants
100ml chicken stock

Method

For the venison

Start the day before by marinating the venison in red wine overnight.

When this is done, heat the oil and butter in a heavy-based frying pan.

When hot, add the venison pieces. Don't shake the pan, just leave them to brown. Turn the pieces in the order in which you put them in, that way you'll get consistently cooked medallions. When the blood starts to pierce the surface, transfer them to another dish and place in a very low oven to keep warm.

For the blackcurrant sauce

Pour off any fat left in the pan, but retain the sediment to make the sauce. Add the red wine, port, blackcurrant juice and crème de cassis and season with a few twists of black pepper.

Bring it to a rapid boil. As it starts to reduce you may add a little more wine, port or juice to taste. Cook until it reduces by about half and has thickened nicely, then add the chicken stock to the sauce and taste.

Leave to gently simmer for at least 2 hours.

Finish the sauce with a splash of cream, just to stabilise it. You could also add a bit of vinegar to the sauce to sharpen it if need be but blackcurrants can be quite acidic, so it may not be necessary. Add the blackcurrants to the sauce to warm them through gently.

To serve

Place the venison pieces in a serving dish and pour over the red wine and fresh blackcurrant sauce. Garnish as in picture.

THE "BEES KNEES" CHEESECAKE

SERVES 8

Muscat De Rivesaltes,
Chateau de Jau

Ingredients

Base

50g butter melted
125g digestive biscuits (crushed)

Filling

3 x 200g packs of Philadelphia cream cheese
150g caster sugar
3 large eggs
3 large egg yolks
175ml soured cream
1½ tbsp vanilla essence
1½ tbsp lemon juice

Method

Preheat oven to 180°C and boil a kettle of water.

For the base

Mix the melted butter with the crushed biscuits and press them into the bottom of the tin to make a firm base of about 5mm depth.

Sit the tin on a piece of kitchen foil large enough to form a waterproof wrapping around the tin. Press the foil around the tin and place the wrapped tin in the fridge.

For the filling

Beat the cream cheese in a food processor until smooth, then add the sugar and mix it thoroughly.

Next add the eggs and egg yolks one at a time. When the eggs are fully incorporated add the soured cream, vanilla and lemon juice and process until smooth and creamy.

To assemble

Take the tin out of the fridge and place in a roasting tin. Fill the cake tin with the mixture and pour the boiled water into the roasting tin to a depth of about 5cm.

Place the roasting tin in the oven for about an hour, or until the cheesecake has browned slightly around the edges and the centre is set.

Take the cheesecake out of the water bath and leave to cool, then place it (still in the foil wrapping) in the fridge. It will continue to cook as it cools and it will firm up further in the fridge.

To serve

Assemble as in the picture.

120
MICHAEL CAINES
AT ABODE CHESTER

Grosvener Road, Chester CH1 2DJ

01244 347 000
www.abodehotels.co.uk

The Michael Caines Restaurant at ABode Chester offers Michael's award winning, modern European cuisine in a stylish 5th-floor setting with fantastic views overlooking Chester racecourse and the Welsh hills. Michael Caines, the two-star Michelin chef from Gidleigh Park, Dartmoor, has brought his distinctive style of cuisine and dining to the Northwest: at once classic, yet innovative, modern and never overly formal. In addition to the full à la carte and tasting menus, the Michael Caines Restaurant features Michael's exciting grazing menus: small and beautifully presented dishes that can also be enjoyed more informally in the stylish Champagne Bar. The 'Amazing Graze' lunch changes weekly, an outstanding value menu with the option of matched wines.

Stuart Collins is Michael's talented Executive Chef. Stuart gained his first professional job at the Michael Caines Restaurant at ABode Exeter. He then moved to Gidleigh Park, learning his profession under Michael's direct two-star Michelin tutelage. These three formative years were very important to him.

"Michael runs a very calm, well disciplined kitchen and working at Gidleigh Park taught me cooking at the highest level," says Stuart.

When Gidleigh Park closed for its year-long refurbishment, Stuart moved to Gordon Ramsay's flagship restaurant on Royal Hospital Road, London.

After 18 months there, he had the opportunity to move to New York and assist in the opening of Gordon Ramsay's restaurant at The London Hotel. From there, he was appointed Head Chef at Maze, where he helped to bring to America the concept of grazing menus.

The Michael Caines Restaurant is the spectacular centrepiece of the ABode Chester dining experience. Located on the 5th floor, with wonderful views of the surrounding countryside, this is a special place to come to enjoy Michael Caines cuisine of the highest order

CITRUS CURED SALMON, LOBSTER MAYONNAISE, AVOCADO PUREE, SWEET LEMON, GINGER CRISP

SERVES 4

Reserve de Gassac Viognier 2010 – Vin de Pays de l'Hérault, Languedoc-Roussillon, France

Ingredients

Salmon
200g salmon fillet, pin boned and skinned
2 lemons
2 limes
100g curing salt
100g chervil (finely chopped)

Avocado Puree
1 avocado

Ginger Crisp
100g ginger root
500ml stock syrup
500ml vegetable oil

Lobster Mayonnaise
100ml mayonnaise
20ml lobster stock reduction

Vinaigrette
50g celery
50g cucumber
50g confit lemon
100ml olive oil vinaigrette
micro herbs

Method

For the salmon
Zest the lemons and limes. Mix the zest with the curing salt and sprinkle over the salmon. Allow to cure for 40 minutes. Wash off the salt and zest using water. Gently steam the salmon for 1 ½ minutes on both sides and cover in clingfilm. Allow to cool for 10 minutes and, using clingfilm, roll in the chopped chervil.

For the avocado puree
Cut the avocado in half, remove the stone and scrape out the avocado flesh. Place into a blender and squeeze in the juice of 1 lime, add a pinch of salt, and blend until smooth.

For the ginger crisp
Peel the ginger root. Thinly slice and gently cook the ginger in stock syrup for about 1 hour. Remove from the stock syrup and place into a pan of vegetable oil at 160°C. Fry for 5 minutes until golden. Remove from the oil and place on parchment paper, the ginger will crisp as it cools.

For the lobster mayonnaise
Fold the lobster reduction through the mayonnaise until smooth, adjust the flavour using the lemon juice and salt.

For the vinaigrette
Add the celery, cucumber and lemon dice into a bowl. Then add vinaigrette and approx 50ml of the cooking liquor from the lemons. Season the mix with salt and pepper and finish with the chopped chervil.

To serve
Slice the salmon into 2cm pieces and remove the clingfilm. Pipe the lobster mayonnaise and avocado puree onto the plate. Finish the dish with the vinaigrette and crisp ginger.

GOOSNARGH DUCK BREAST, CONFIT LEG WITH APRICOTS AND PISTACHIO, SWEET POTATOES, SPROUTING BROCCOLI

SERVES 4

Salentein Reserve Pinot Noir 2008, Valle de Uco, Argentina

Ingredients

Duck Breast

4 duck breasts

Confit Leg with Apricots and Pistachios

4 duck legs
50g coarse sea salt
15g whole black peppercorns (crushed)
15g whole white peppercorns (crushed)
2 garlic cloves (peeled and sliced)
4 sprigs of thyme (large)
4 bay leafs
2 litre duck fat
50g pistachio nuts
50g apricots (diced small)
15g rosemary (chopped)
15g sage (chopped)
50g rye bread croutons

Sweet Potato Fondants

4 large sweet potatoes
2 thyme sprigs
3 cloves of garlic

Sprouting Broccoli

300g sprouting broccoli

Five Spice Sauce

300ml duck jus
200ml veal glace
300ml chicken stock
1 large onions (cut into thick rings)
1 head of garlic (cut in half)
30ml xeres (sherry) vinegar
10g fresh thyme
30g cream
3g Chinese five spice
80g honey (clear)

Method

For the confit leg with apricots and pistachios

Mix the salt with the crushed peppercorns. Onto a small tray, scatter over ½ of the salt and pepper, then place the duck legs on top and scatter the rest of the salt and pepper over the duck legs.

Crumble over the thyme, bay leaves and add the sliced garlic. Seal with clingfilm and marinade for 12 hours. Once marinated, wash off the legs with water and dry on a cloth. Heat the duck fat to 80°C and add the legs, gently confit the leg until soft and tender for about 2 to 3 hours.

Leave to cool in the fat, then pick the meat away from the bone and fold through the apricots, pistachios, herbs and croutons. Adjust its flavour with salt and pepper.

Roll flat between two pieces of parchment paper and chill. Cut into the size and shape required.

For the sweet potato fondants and broccoli

Cut the sweet potatoes into the required shape.

Using a heavy bottom pan, add a little butter and then the thyme and garlic, place the potatoes into the pan and colour on all sides. Add more butter and cook on a medium heat until the potato is soft. Allow to rest in the butter. Boil the broccoli for 3 minutes.

For the five spice sauce

Bring the duck just to the boil, and mix in the 5 spice.

Separately, in a saucepan we are going to make a gastric with the honey and vinegar.

Heat the honey, bring it to a rolling boil and cook for 3 minutes, but be careful not to burn the honey. Add the vinegar and reduce to nothing. Now add to the chicken stock, veal glace, peppercorns, thyme and cream.

Bring to the boil and skim, reduce to a simmer and cook out for 30 minutes. Strain through a colander and then pass through a fine sieve. Reduce to consistency required; adjust the seasoning and the acidity.

To serve

Sear the duck breast on a medium heat, rendering the fat. Drain off any excess fat and return to heat. Cook for about 5 minutes on the skin side and turn over. The skin should be golden brown. Cook for a further 2 minutes and remove from the pan. Allow to rest for 5 minutes. Place the confit leg mix onto a warm plate, allowing to warm through. Re-heat the fondant potatoes and broccoli, place onto plate. Carve the duck and lie on top of the confit leg. Finish the plate with the five spice sauce.

MOJITO

SERVES 4

🍷 *Jurançon 2008, Domaine Castera, Jurançon, France*

Ingredients

Muscavado Jelly

440g Muscavado sugar
1 litre water
19g gelatine

Lime Syrup

300ml lime juice
10g pectin
100g sugar

Lime Yoghurt

600ml yoghurt
45g icing sugar
135ml lime syrup (as above)
1 vanilla pod (scraped)

Mint and Lime Granite

500ml water
75g sugar
50g mint
3 limes (juiced)

Rum Syrup

50ml rum
100ml stock syrup
60 lime juice

Candied Mint

mint leaves
egg white
caster sugar

Method

For the muscavado jelly

Add the sugar and water together in a pan and bring to the boil. Bloom the gelatine and add to the water and sugar, pass and cool until required.

For the lime syrup

Heat the lime juice to 40°C and add the sugar and pectin. Bring to the boil and remove from the heat. Reserve for later use.

For the lime yoghurt

Sieve the icing sugar into the yoghurt, fold through the vanilla and lime syrup until even mix.

For the mint and lime granite

Add all ingredients into a pan, bring to the boil and remove from the heat. Cover with clingfilm and allow to stand for 30 minutes. Pass through a fine sieve and freeze. Once frozen, scrape with a fork to make the granite.

For the rum syrup

Mix the rum, stock syrup and lime juice together.

For the candied mint

Brush each leaf with egg white and sprinkle with caster sugar. Allow to dry for approx 6 hours.

To serve

Set a thin layer of the Muscavado jelly in the bottom of the glass, pour the lime yoghurt on top, place the granite crystals on top of the yoghurt. Finish with the candied mint and serve the syrup on the side to be poured table side.

130
MICHAEL CAINES
AT ABODE MANCHESTER

107 Piccadilly, Manchester M1 2BD

0161 200 5678
www.abodehotels.co.uk

Since opening in 2008, the Michael Caines Restaurant at ABode Manchester has established itself as one of Manchester's most exciting dining destinations. Just minutes from bustling Piccadilly in a period Victorian cotton merchant's warehouse, the Restaurant and Champagne Bar are located in an atmospheric lower-level dining room that is stylish and discreet.

Michael Caines, the two-star Michelin chef from Gidleigh Park, Dartmoor, has brought his innovative style of modern European cuisine to Manchester. It is here that he pioneered his grazing concept, creating menus of small-size dishes that are big on flavour and presentation and which allow diners to eat as much or as little as they like. The grazing menu is available in the Champagne Bar as well as in the Restaurant and there is a weekly-changing 'Amazing Graze' lunch menu that is probably the best value lunch in Manchester.

ABode Manchester's Executive Chef is Mark Rossi. Mark knows Michael and his distinctive style of cuisine well, having worked previously under the maestro at Gidleigh Park and as Executive Chef at the Michael Caines Restaurant at ABode Canterbury. Mark is a brilliant chef in his own right.

In addition to working with Michael, he has worked with Nico Ladenis at 3-star Michelin Chez Nico and with the Roux brothers at the famous 3-star Waterside Inn. A stint with Phil Howard at the 2-star Michelin The Square added to his classical training and knowledge. In Manchester, Mark is enjoying making use of the best local and regional produce and ingredients from Manchester, Lancashire, Cheshire and surrounds.

The Michael Caines Restaurant and Champagne Bar at ABode Manchester serves exciting and innovative European cuisine utilising the best local and regional produce. Executive Chef Mark Rossi, in consultation with Michael Caines, has created an exciting range of menus including grazing, a la carte and tasting

PAN-FRIED SCALLOPS WITH PEA PUREE AND A SHALLOT AND SMOKED BACON VELOUTE

SERVES 2

Toques et Clochers Chardonnay 2008, Limoux, France

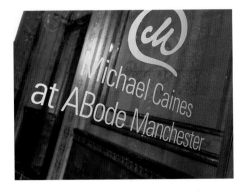

Ingredients

8 large scallops
micro herbs (to dress)
olive oil
5ml lemon juice

Pea Puree

500g frozen peas
50g butter
salt and pepper

Shallot and Bacon Veloute

250g shallots (sliced)
300g fish stock
200g smoked bacon trimmings
50ml cream
250ml milk
70g butter
1 bay leaf
1 sprig of thyme (large)
salt and pepper

Method

For the veloute

Pre-heat the oven to 200°C. First, place the bacon trimmings and the milk together in a saucepan and bring to the boil. Separately, sweat the shallots with butter and a pinch of salt and cook until soft and transparent. Then add the thyme and bay leaf and continue to sweat for a further 2 minutes. Next, add the fish stock, cream and the infused milk with the bacon trimmings, bring to the boil and simmer for 20 minutes. Then remove the bacon trimmings, thyme and bay leaf and pour the liquid and shallots into a blender. Blend until very smooth. Pass through a fine sieve. Set aside until required.

When ready to serve, gently warm the veloute, season with salt and pepper and add a knob of butter then create a cappuccino effect using a hand blender.

For the pea puree

Next, cook the peas in boiling salted water until soft, then remove from the water and refresh in iced water. Once cool, strain off the water and leave the peas to drain for a little while. Place 400g into a food processor, blend to a puree, then pass the puree through a sieve to remove the outer skins. Warm the puree in a saucepan and mix in the butter, then season with salt and pepper. Add the remaining peas just before serving.

For the scallops

Now cook the scallops. Season with salt and pepper on both sides and place the scallops into a non-stick pan with a little oil. Then place into the pre-heated oven for 2 minutes on each side, being careful not to overcook. Now remove from the oven and squeeze lemon juice over the fish.

To serve

Place a tier of pea puree onto a plate and place the scallops onto the puree. Spoon the froth from the sauce around the fish, dress with some micro herbs and serve. Bon appetit!

BEEF FILLET OF DARTMOOR WITH TRUFFLE POMME PUREE, RAGOUT OF WILD MUSHROOMS, BROAD BEANS, ASPARAGUS

SERVES 2

Tour des Gendres Bergerac 2007, Malbec / Merlot, Bergerac, France

Ingredients

2 x160g wild fillet beef (untrimmed)
150g truffled potato puree
100g asparagus
80g wild mushroom and broad bean ragout
200g fresh spinach
60ml beef Maderia sauce
200ml chicken stock

Confit of Chopped Shallots

12g shallots (chopped)

Truffled Potato Puree

100g Binjte potatoes
20ml full fat milk
5ml black truffle oil
2g black truffles

Beef Maderia Sauce

130g beef trimmings stock
90ml chicken stock
50ml five year old Madeira brandy
25ml veal glace
20g shallots
10ml double cream
10ml sherry vinegar
5g garlic

Veal Glace

12g veal rib bones
5g tomato puree
5ml white cooking wine
15g carrots, Spanish onions and leeks
5g celery
10g plain flour

Wild Mushroom and Broad Bean Ragout

20g broad beans
15g confit of chopped shallots
15g of each of the following mushrooms - girolles, pied blue, pied de mouton, skitake, oyster, cepes

Method

For the confit of shallots

Finely chop the shallots. Wash off in a sieve and dry with a cloth. Melt the butter in a saucepan and add the chopped shallots and thyme. Confit slowly for 30 minutes, stirring time-to-time and adding a drop of water when needed. When they show no colour, strain off the excess butter and reserve for later use.

For the truffled pomme puree

Place the potatoes into a saucepan and cover with the water, add salt to taste, bring to the boil and reduce to a simmer. Once completely cooked, but not over cooked, strain the potatoes through a sieve and allow to air dry for 3 minutes. Pass through a fine sieve into a bowl. Heat the butter and milk and whisk into the passed potatoes. Clingfilm the bowl and keep in a warm place until needed.

To finish add truffle jus, oil and chopped truffle to taste.

For the beef madeira sauce

In a roasting tray on top of the oven, heat the oil and add the beef trimmings, seal well. Add the butter and caramelise until lightly brown. Now add shallots and sweat until they have no colour. Add the sliced mushrooms and sweat until slippery in look. Deglace with sherry vinegar and reduce by half, now add the maderia and truffle marinade. Reduce by half and add the remaining ingredients. Bring to the boil and transfer to a saucepan. Then bring back to the boil, skim, and reduce to a simmer. Cook out for 45 minutes to 1 hr, then pass through a colander and fine chinoise. Reduce the consistency, season lightly and pass through muslin cloth. Reserve until needed.

For the veal glace

Lightly roast off the bones turning from time-to-time. For the last 10 minutes, sprinkle with the flour and finish roasting. Place the bones into the stockpot once roasted. In a large saucepan, sweat the vegetables in the oil, but do not colour. Add the white wine and reduce by half then add the tomato paste. Leave to compote for 30 minutes and then add to the bones. Fill the stockpot with water, to just above the level of the bones and bring to the boil. Skim the stock and then reduce to a simmer. Leave to cookout for 24 hours and then pass off through a colander and reduce. Pass through a chinoise and leave to cool.

To serve

Place the puree on the plate, with the mushroom and broad bean ragout in the middle, place the beef on the beans topped with the confit of shallots. Add sauce as desired.

TRIO OF CHOCOLATE

SERVES 8

Banyuls Rimage 2008, Les Clos de Paulilles,
Banyuls, France

Ingredients

Hazelnut Nougatine

400g hazelnuts
1kg caster sugar
500ml liquid glucose

Pâté à Bomber

150g caster sugar
60ml water
12 egg yolks

Italian Meringue

75g caster sugar
75ml liquid glucose
30g water
10 egg whites (whipped to a stiff peak)
50g frangelico
200g hazelnut praline milk chocolate (melted)
150ml double cream (whipped)
100g milk chocolate (roughly chopped)
125g hazelnut nougatine (see above)
8 chocolate tear moulds

Chocolate Ganache

2 eggs
160ml milk
400ml cream
400g dark chocolate (melted)

100g chocolate sable
300g white chocolate ice cream

Method

For the hazelnut nougatine

Roast the hazelnuts in a preheated oven at 200°C and remove the skins. Heat the sugar and the glucose on medium heat. When the sugar starts to turn gold, add the hazelnuts and mix. Pour on a non stick tray and leave to cool before blitzing everything in a food processor.

For the pâté à bomber

Make a syrup by bringing the sugar and the water up to 120°C. Whisk the egg yolks until they are creamy and pour in the syrup while whisking until the mixture cools.

For the meringue

Bring the sugar, glucose and water up to 120°C. Whip the egg whites until they become firm and add the syrup, mixing until it cools. Next add the frangelico and the melted hazelnut chocolate to the pâté à bomber mixture. Then fold in the whipped cream, meringue, milk chocolate and hazelnuts nougatine. Fill an individual pot with the mixture and put in the freezer until ready to serve.

For the chocolate ganache

Place the eggs into a jug. Put the milk and cream in a saucepan over a medium heat and bring to the boil. Then, using a stick whisk, pour the boiling milk and cream onto the eggs, blending as you do so. Stir the mixture into the melted chocolate, using a whisk at first and then a wooden spoon. Line 8 x 4cm rings with clingfilm, pour the warm ganache mixture into these and put them in the fridge for a minimum of 2 hours, until the ganache has set.

To serve

Take the ganache rings out of the fridge and leave to one side until they reach room temperature. Then take the parfait out of their teardrop moulds and put one on each of your plates. Loosen the ganache from the rings (either by heating the outside of the rings, briefly, with a culinary blow torch, or by carefully running a knife around the edges of the ganache), then pop them out and place each one on a sablé biscuit. Transfer the biscuits to the plates, add a scoop of white chocolate ice-cream and serve.

Chef's tip

Always melt chocolate in a bowl placed over a saucepan of simmering water (a bain-marie) but don't let the water touch the bowl.

140
NUTTERS
RESTAURANT

Edenfield Road, Norden, Rochdale OL12 7TT

01706 650 167
www.nuttersrestaurant.co.uk

Nutters Restaurant is housed in the lavish grounds of an 18th century manor house; 6 ½ acres of groomed parkland with spectacular views across Ashworth Moors, Greater Manchester and beyond. It is the perfect setting for the extravagance and elegance of Andrew Nutter's cuisine. His cooking is unique; an indulgent explosion of the senses that is based on the very best of local and regional produce and is exemplified by Andrew's stunning, award winning Crispy Black Pudding Wontons, his Roast Line Caught Seabass with Tempura Vegetables and Ponzu Dressing, and the Dark Chocolate and Strawberry Chip Soufflé Pudding, a truly decadent dessert.

Despite the wider success of Andrew's cooking, Nutter's Restaurant has remained very much a family affair. Jean Nutter, Andrew's mum, does the accounts and administration whilst his dad, Rodney Nutter, looks after both the management of the business and the restaurant's wines and spirits operation.

The main restaurant seats 150 diners with additional dining in the private rooms accommodating up to 120 guests, providing the perfect venue for Civil Wedding Ceremonies, cocktail parties and lavish receptions. Whether it's a light lunch, romantic dinner or sumptuous afternoon tea, a Nutter meal is always an experience of interesting flavours and unusual combinations, but above all it's a meal to be enjoyed in beautiful surroundings, safe in the confidence of the quality of the ingredients and the attentiveness of the staff.

Dazzling local ingredients with
the eclectic mix of Nutter's
flavours hit the palette
like a kaleidoscope, changing
and morphing with each bite

BRILL WITH ROAST PEPPER CRUST, SEARED SCALLOPS AND BURY BLACK PUDDING

SERVES 2

🍷 *Domaine de Vedilhan Serica, Viognier 2009*

Ingredients

Red Pepper Crust

1 red pepper (roasted till golden brown, skinned and de-seeded)
1 clove garlic
50g dry white breadcrumbs
50g parmesan cheese
50g butter

Chive Butter Sauce

50ml white wine
50ml white wine vinegar
50ml whipping cream
100g chilled butter (cubed)
1 tbsp chives (chopped)

Fish

2 tbsp olive oil
2 x 180g fillets of brill (skinned and boned)

Black Pudding and Scallops

splash olive oil
10 slices Bury black pudding
10 scallops (diver caught if possible)
25g fresh samphire
pinch 5 spice powder

Method

For the red pepper crumb

Blend the pepper flesh and garlic together until smooth. Add the breadcrumbs, parmesan cheese and butter and blend them to a paste. Place on a sheet of greaseproof paper, cover with another piece, and roll until it is 2mm thick. Then cut into squares and place in a fridge to firm.

For the chive butter sauce

Place the wine and vinegar in a small pan and reduce it by half, then add the cream and reduce again. Slowly add the butter, whisking as you do until emulsified. Season to taste and keep warm.

For the fish

Firstly, heat the olive oil in a non-stick pan. Then season the fish and seal presentation side down first until golden brown, and turn over and seal the other side. Remove the fish from the pan, top with the crust and place in a hot oven at 180°C to cook through.

For the bury black pudding and scallops

When ready to serve, drizzle olive oil over the black pudding slices and place in the oven to heat through.

Place the non-stick pan back on the heat then add some more olive oil and seal the scallops until golden on both sides. Remove them from the pan and add the samphire and 5 spice powder then toss briefly.

To serve

Once all the components are hot and ready, arrange the black pudding and scallops on a plate, then add the samphire and top with the brill. Finally, add the chives to the sauce and spoon it around the plate.

HONEY ROAST GOOSNARGH DUCK BREAST WITH SZECHUAN PEPPER AND GINGER

SERVES 4

Old Vine Grenache, Clarendon Hills – Kangarilla 1999

Ingredients

2 Goosnargh ducks weighing approx 2kg each (legs and breast removed)
2 tbsp salt
500ml goose fat

Szechuan Dust

1 tsp toasted sesame oil
2 tsp Szechuan peppercorns
pinch dried chilli flakes
4 garlic cloves (chopped)
1 tsp sesame seeds
1 tsp poppy seeds
4 spring onions (finely chopped)

Pak Choi Stir Fry

4 heads pak choi
2 tbsp olive oil
1 banana shallot (finely shredded)
1 clove garlic (finely chopped)
1 red chilli (finely chopped)
1 small knob of fresh ginger (finely chopped)
few leaves fresh coriander (chopped)
squeezed fresh lime
pinch 5 spice powder

Duck Breast

4 duck breasts
4 tbsp runny honey

Ginger Sauce

1 knob butter
1 shallot (finely chopped)
1 small knob ginger (finely chopped)
300ml red wine
300ml strong beef stock

Method

For the duck legs

Take the duck legs and rub them with salt, then cover and leave overnight. Wash off the salt, pat dry, then place them in a small roasting tray, covered with goose fat. Place in an oven at 120°C and cook for 2 hours 30 minutes or until tender. Cool slightly, and then remove all the bones apart from the presentation one. Then place in the fridge until ready to use.

For the szechuan dust

Place the sesame oil, Szechuan peppercorns, chilli flakes, garlic, sesame seeds and poppy seeds into the pestle and mortar and grind them into a powder. Place this in a small frying pan and toast it lightly, then add the spring onions and slightly wilt them.

For the pak choi

Remove a few leaves from each one and blanch for 2 seconds to wilt, then reserve until later. Finely shred the remaining pak choi. Heat the olive oil and fry half off the shallot, garlic, chilli and ginger for 2 minutes, then add half of the pak choi, coriander, lime and a pinch of 5 spice. Wilt it slightly, then cool. Take a sheet of clingfilm and place some of the reserved blanched pak choi on top. Then add some of the wilted pak choi and with the help of the food wrap form it into a ball.

For the ginger sauce

Heat the butter in a small pan, add the shallot and ginger and sweat gently for 5 minutes until softened. Add the red wine and reduce by half, then add the beef stock and continue reducing until slightly thickened.

To finish

When ready to serve, place the duck legs on a tray and roast in a hot oven at 180°C for about 10 minutes until hot and golden. Heat a frying pan, season the duck breasts and fry fat side down until golden brown, then turn over and seal the other side. Remove from the pan, drain off any excess fat and add the honey, cook until a light golden colour then spoon some of the honey over the duck breasts. Place in a hot oven 180°C and cook for 6 minutes then remove from the oven. Cover and leave to rest.

To serve

When ready to plate up, reheat the pak choi balls by placing them on a small, buttered tray cover with foil then place in the oven. Place the remaining stir fry mixture into a frying pan and wilt. Season to taste.

Arrange the pak choi on a plate then slice the duck and fan it out slightly. Arrange the duck leg, pak choi ball and starch of your choice, and then spoon on some of the sauce. Finish with a scattering of the Szechuan dust.

RASPBERRY AND WHITE CHOCOLATE CHEESECAKES

SERVES 6

🍷 *Banyuls, Leon Parce, Domaine de la Rectorie,*
Roussillon 2007

Method

For the base

Mix together the biscuits and butter and press them into six individual metal rings. Place in fridge to firm.

For the cheesecake mix

Gently mix together the mascarpone and sugar, fold in the whipped cream and then quickly fold in the melted chocolate. Spoon the mixture over the bases and smooth it out to just under the rim. Place in the fridge until firm.

For the raspberry jelly

Warm the raspberry coulis and add the soaked gelatine, then stir until it dissolves. Cool slightly, then pour this on top of the cheesecakes and put them back in the fridge to set. With the remaining jelly, pour it into small ice cube trays and also place in the fridge.

To serve

Remove the cheesecakes from the rings and place on decorated plates. Add the jellys, raspberries, mint and finish with a flourish of chocolate decorations and ice cream.

Ingredients

Base

200g custard cream biscuits (crushed)
50g melted butter

Cheesecake Mix

250g mascarpone cream cheese
25g caster sugar
175g whipping cream (whipped)
175g white chocolate (melted)

Raspberry Jelly

250ml raspberry coulis
2 leaves of soaked gelatine

Garnish

fresh raspberries
mint leaves
chocolate decorations
pure vanilla bean ice cream

150
THE PEACOCK ROOM

Crimble Lane, Bamford, Rochdale OL11 4AD

01706 368 591
www.thedeckersgroup.com

The Peacock Room at The Crimble has placed itself amongst the region's fine dining culinary elite.

Head Chef Robert Walker is passionate about the quality of the ingredients he uses, and this includes the superb cuts of meat which are freshly prepared in our butchery department. He works closely with local suppliers to ensure the dishes we serve are to our consistently high standards. The constantly evolving menu encapsulates modern English cuisine, combining traditional flavours with modern techniques.

The extensive wine list will provide you the opportunity to combine our dishes with a variety of wines from around the world. Our dedicated team of friendly staff lead by Restaurant Manager David Bowman-Powell would be pleased to offer advice in making a wine selection to complement your food.

The Peacock Room is located within the Crimble Restaurant complex. Set away from the hustle and bustle of everyday life, in mature gardens with views over the rural landscape. Watch out for the ostentation of peacocks who live and roam freely within the grounds of this beautiful building.

So sit back, relax, and enjoy a glass of champagne or a cocktail in the opulent aperitif bar before entering the luxurious dining room. Two stunning crystal chandeliers, reclaimed from a cruise liner, shine brightly, highlighting the superb attention to detail for which this restaurant has become locally recognised.

So sit back, relax, and enjoy a glass of champagne or a cocktail in the opulent aperitif bar before entering the luxurious dining room

BAKED BEETROOT TART WITH PEPPERED GOATS CHEESE

SERVES 4

 Savennieres, Clos du Papillon, Domaine Baumard

Ingredients

Beetroot Tart

4 large raw beetroot
100g puff pastry
250g salted butter

Pickled Beetroot

2 large golden beetroot
250ml white wine vinegar
100g sugar

Truffle Mayonnaise

200ml mayonnaise
20ml truffle oil

Peppered Goats Cheese

1 Kidderton Ash goats cheese
100g breadcrumbs
100g flour
2 whole eggs
100ml milk
½ teaspoon cracked black pepper

Garnish

beetroot leaves

Method

For the beetroot tart

Wash, peel and slice the beetroot into 4mm slices. Cut out discs of beetroot approximately 3.5cms wide, saving the trimmings.

Melt the butter over a low heat and place the beetroot discs into the butter. Cook at 125°C until completely cooked through. Remove from the tray and do the same with the beetroot trimmings. Once cooked, blend the trimmings to a puree.

Whilst warm, fan the discs out inside a 9-10cm pastry cutter on greaseproof paper and refrigerate.

Roll out the puff pastry to 2mm thick and bake at 180°C for 12 – 14 minutes.

Cut discs from the pastry with the 9-10cm cutter and spoon in the beetroot puree, top with a beetroot disc. Place in a pre- heated oven at 170°C for 7 minutes.

For the pickled beetroot

Wash the golden beetroot then boil it until cooked. Leave to cool slightly, then peel and cut into half cm cubes.

Briefly boil the diced beetroot in the vinegar and sugar. Remove from the heat to cool.

For the truffle mayonnaise

Whisk together mayonnaise and truffle oil. A splash of water will thin the mixture down to a pouring consistency.

For the peppered goats cheese

Remove the rind from the cheese and roughly dice. Add a grind of black pepper then shape into balls.

Place the flour and breadcrumbs into 2 separate bowls and in a third bowl mix together the eggs and milk.

Dip each goats cheese ball into the flour, egg and then the breadcrumb mix. Repeat, then deep fry at 170°C until golden brown.

To serve

Dress the plate with the mayonnaise, the pickled beetroot and beetroot leaves. Remove the tart from the oven, place the goats cheese ball on top and place in the centre of the plate.

GLOUCESTER OLD SPOT PORK FILLET AND BELLY WITH CELERIAC, QUINCE AND CIDER JUS

SERVES 4

🍷 *Premier Cru, Beaune,*
Les Marconnet

Ingredients

2 pork fillet
200g kale

Pork Belly

800g pork belly
2 carrots
2 onions
3 sticks of celery
2 leeks
1 litre veal stock
1 litre cider
1 bulb of garlic
1 bunch of fresh thyme
(Keep some of each to use with the fondant potato)

Sauce

4 shallots
100g quince paste

Fondant Potato

4 large potatoes
400g butter

Celeriac

1 celeriac
200ml cream

Puree

4 fresh quince
150g sugar
200ml water

Roast Vegetable

16 chantenay carrots
2 turnips
2 parsnips

Method

For the pork belly

Roughly chop the carrots, leeks, onion and celery, add half of the garlic and half the thyme, and place into a deep, oven proof dish. Bring the cider up to the boil and reduce by half, add the veal stock and simmer. Season the pork belly and place on top of the vegetables, then pour over the hot stock and place in the oven at 150°C for 3 hours. Leave to cool. Place another tray on top of the belly pork and refrigerate overnight.

For the sauce

Peel and dice the shallots, then caramelise in a saucepan with a clove of garlic and thyme. Strain the stock used to cook the pork belly and pour it onto the shallots. Reduce, then finish with the quince paste. Strain again.

For the fondant potato

Peel the potatoes and cut them into slices about an inch thick using a 5cm pastry cutter. Melt the butter in an ovenproof dish and put in the potatoes, covering them with the butter. Add a sprig of thyme and a clove of garlic and season.

Place in the oven at 170°C until they are cooked.

For the celeriac

Peel and grate the celeriac. Fry it gently in oil until almost cooked, then add the cream and reduce by half.

For the puree

Peel the quince, then quarter it and remove the core, then chop finely. Add the sugar to a shallow pan and heat slowly until golden brown, then add the quince to the pan. Stir in well and cook for 5 minutes, add 200ml water and boil for 5 minutes. Blend until smooth and then pass through a sieve.

For the roast vegetables

Peel all the vegetables and cut them to a similar size. Add a glug of vegetable oil to an ovenproof dish and heat on the hob – add the veg and season. Put in a 160°C oven and turn the vegetables over every ten minutes until tender.

To finish

Pick the kale, boil in salted water for 3 mins and finish in salted butter. Season and pan-fry the pork fillet until evenly coloured. Place in the oven at 160°C for 8 to 10 minutes. Leave to rest for 5 minutes and then slice. Portion the pork belly, and reheat in the oven for 15 minutes. Once hot, coat with sauce to glaze.

To serve

Dress the plate with the puree, potatoes and vegetables and finally the meat and sauce.

DARK CHOCOLATE DELICE WITH AMARETTO ICE CREAM, TOASTED PISTACHIOS AND ESPRESSO FOAM

SERVES 4

 Nederburg Noble Late Harvest

Ingredients

Delice

160ml milk
70ml cream
1 egg
170g dark chocolate

Flapjack

50g sugar
40ml water
220g porridge oats
150g brown sugar
½ vanilla pod
150g melted butter

Amaretto Ice Cream

500ml milk
170ml cream
4 egg yolks
135g sugar
1 vanilla pod
50ml amaretto

Caramel Syrup

100g sugar
70ml water

Chocolate Tuille

30ml water
150g glucose
150g sugar
20g cocoa powder

Espresso Foam

250ml espresso
2 sheets of gelatine

Toasted Pistachios

100g pistachios
60g butter
50g caster sugar

Method

For the flapjack

Place the water and sugar in a pan and cook until light brown in colour. Pour into a mixing bowl and add the porridge oats, brown sugar and vanilla then the melted butter and mix. Spread the mix onto a baking tray approx 5mm thick and bake at 170°C for 10 – 12 minutes. Once cooled, break into small pieces and sprinkle into a baking tin with a removable base. You may only need half the mix so the rest could be eaten as biscuits.

For the delice

Bring the milk and cream to the boil and while it is heating, whisk the egg until light and fluffy. Then pour the milk and cream onto the egg, stir and return to the pan and cook until just about to boil. Remove from the heat and add the chocolate, stir, until fully mixed. Pour the mixture on top of the flapjack base and place in the fridge to chill.

For the amaretto ice cream

Put the milk, cream and vanilla into a saucepan and bring to the boil. While it is heating, put the egg yolks and sugar into a bowl and whisk together lightly. Once the milk and cream has boiled, pour it over the egg mixture, mix, then return to the pan and cook until thickened but do not boil. Add the amaretto and then chill. Once chilled churn in an ice cream machine and place in the freezer.

For the chocolate tuille

Bring the water, sugar and glucose to the boil and cook until 160°C. Add the cocoa and mix quickly, then pour onto a heatproof mat and leave to cool. Once cooled, place another heatproof mat on top and put into the oven at 160°C for 7 minutes. With care, remove the top mat and pull the sugar into long strands and leave to cool, they should now be crisp.

For the caramel syrup

Mix the sugar with 30ml of water and boil until light brown in colour. Add the rest of the water and pour into a small bowl to chill.

For the espresso foam

Soak the gelatine until soft then add to the warm coffee. Froth using a small hand blender.

For the toasted pistachios

Melt the butter in a frying pan until it foams and add the nuts, stirring continuously until the nuts are lightly browned. Sieve then mix with the sugar.

To serve

Slice the delice and arrange on a plate with the pistachios, foam and ice cream.

160
THE PLOUGH & FLAIL

Paddock Hill, Mobberley, Cheshire WA16 7DB

01565 873 537
www.thedeckersgroup.com

Welcome to Cheshire's worst kept secret! The Plough & Flail has become loved for the superb quality of food and high caliber of customer service. Set this in a beautiful pub, expertly finished to a majestic standard in rural countryside, and you have a venue which we are all very proud of.

Head Chef Nick Wolter sets the tone in the kitchen, assisted by Sous Chef Carl Jenkins, creating a frequently changing menu and selection of blackboard specials. The food combines traditional pub dishes, prepared to restaurant quality standards, with more modern British dishes designed to show off the best seasonal produce available. The majority of our meats are freshly prepared in our very own butchery, delivered daily to the exacting standards of our chefs.

Complement your meal with one of our locally produced, hand-pulled guest ales, or choose a bottle of wine from our carefully selected list. You could even visit our purpose built wine cube to view the wines available, and discuss your selection with one of our friendly members of staff.

With extensive outdoor dining facilities, including heated terraces covered by glass canopies, you can enjoy being outdoors even on cooler days. This includes the kitchen garden, where herbs are picked daily for use in our dishes.

Whether you dine in the bar, in the garden room, or outdoors, we are sure you will enjoy the Plough & Flail as much as we do.

With extensive outdoor dining facilities, including heated terraces covered by glass canopies, you can enjoy being outdoors even on cooler days

SEAFOOD SHARING PLATTER

SERVES 2

🍷 *Gavi, Cantina Santa Vittoria,*
Italy

Ingredients

Sea Trout and Beetroot Gravadlax

750g sea trout (unskinned)
1 large bunch of dill (roughly chopped)
50g caster sugar
100g sea salt
2 tbsp white wine vinegar
1 tsp white pepper
1 tbsp Dijon mustard
50g beetroot (grated)

Mackerel Roll Mops

1 whole mackerel (filleted)
150ml pickling vinegar
500ml white wine vinegar
500g caster sugar
1 chilli (deseeded and finely chopped)
20 black peppercorns (crushed)
100g dill
1 small onion (finely sliced)
2 celery stalks (sliced)
1 carrot peeled and (sliced)

Pickled Cucumber

50ml of the pickling vinegar from the roll mops
1 cucumber (peeled into ribbons)

Morecambe Bay Potted Shrimps

50g brown shrimps
1 knob butter
pinch cayenne pepper
pinch of mace
coarse sea salt
white pepper (freshly ground)
juice of half a lemon

80g smoked halibut

Method

For the sea trout and beetroot gravadlax

Place the fish skin-side down on a large piece of clingfilm, place all the other ingredients on top and wrap it up. Place in the fridge and leave with a weight on top to press the fish flat.

For the mackerel roll mops

Boil the vinegar for 3 minutes, then add the remaining ingredients and simmer for 3 more minutes. Then chill overnight. Roll and skewer the mackerel fillets, then add them to the vinegar and refrigerate for 2-3 days.

For the pickled cucumber

Leave the cucumber to pickle in 50ml of the pickling vinegar used in the roll mops.

For the morecambe bay potted shrimps

Melt the butter in a pan and add the remaining ingredients. When the shrimps are cooked, check the seasoning, pour into serving dishes and chill.

For the home smoked halibut

Cure the halibut the same way as the sea trout gravadlax but without the dill and beetroot, then smoke over oak chippings, allow to cool, and slice finely.

To serve

Assemble as in the picture.

LAMB CUTLETS, SLOW BRAISED SHOULDER OF LAMB, WITH HOT POT POTATOES, BROAD BEANS AND MINT JELLY

SERVES 6

🍷 *Canonbah Bridge Shiraz/Grenache/Mouvedre, Australia*

Ingredients

Braised Lamb

1 small shoulder of lamb
5 pints chicken stock
500ml red wine
2 carrots (peeled, cut length ways)
2 sticks celery (halved)
1 leek (roughly chopped)
1 onion (diced)
1 small bunch of thyme
1 stick of rosemary
5 bay leaves
4 garlic cloves (crushed)
salt and pepper
12 lamb chops

Mint Jelly

4 sheets of gelatine
1 pint of mineral water
12 mint leaves
150g caster sugar

Vegetables

6 baby carrots
1 bunch of asparagus
6 baby fennel
250g broad beans (peeled)
butter

Hot Pot Potatoes

200g lamb shoulder (thinly sliced)
(All the vegetables need to be sliced about 2-3 mm thick)
1kg potatoes
1 large carrot
1 leek
1 large shallot
1 tsp thyme & 1 tsp rosemary (chopped)
100ml chicken or lamb stock
butter for greasing
250ml port

Method

For the lamb

Place the shoulder of lamb, in a large oven-proof dish and add all the other ingredients. Add a little salt and pepper, not too much as the stock is reduced at the end to make the jus. Cover tightly with foil and place in the bottom of the oven at around 120°C for 4-5 hours. When the meat is cool enough to handle, pick it off the bone and place on a 60cm square of clingfilm. Place the lamb in the center, form it into a large sausage shape and wrap the clingfilm around it. Tie each end until it is tight, chill, and place in the fridge for at least 4 hours or ideally overnight. Slice the shoulder into 2-3 inch pieces then remove the clingfilm. Place on a greased tray along with the hotpot. Brush with butter and place in a 160°C oven for 8 minutes until hot.

For the port sauce

Strain the braising liquor and skim off any fat, then reduce the volume by simmering until there is 250ml left. Add a large glass of port and reduce again by half. Add 1 tbsp of redcurrant jelly, adjust the seasoning and set aside.

For the hot pot potatoes

Grease a 3 inch ring or ramekin, cover the sides and base by overlapping the sliced potatoes inside the ring. Layer the rest of the ingredients up, seasoning as you go. When then mould is full, press down firmly and pour on the stock. Bake in the oven for approx 50 minutes, until the potatoes are cooked through. Chill and set aside.

For the mint jelly

Melt the gelatine in the heated mineral water with the sugar and the mint leaves. Place the mixture in ice cube trays and refrigerate until set.

For the vegetables

Boil and blanch the vegetables for 2 minutes, then put them straight into iced water. Toss the vegetables in the butter to warm them through and season.

To assemble

Slice the shoulder into 2-3 inch pieces. Remove the clingfilm and place on a greased tray along with the pie. Brush with butter and place in the oven at 160°C for 8 minutes or until hot. Season the chops and brush with oil, char-grill or pan-fry for 3 minutes each side.

To serve

Place the shoulder and hotpot potatoes on the plate. Place the chops on the side. Top with the vegetables and spoon over the sauce. Add a cube of mint jelly.

STRAWBERRY BAVAROIS WITH STRAWBERRY PARFAIT

SERVES 6

*Boizel Rose Brut
Champagne*

Method

For the bavarois

Soak the gelatine in cold water until soft. While this is happening, whisk the eggs and sugar together. Then boil the milk and add the softened gelatin.

Next, fold the milk and egg mixture together. Then add the puree and fold in the cream.

Line the ring with halved strawberries and fill with the bavarois mix. Chill for 3 hours.

For the parfait

Boil the sugar and water to 120°C. Whisk the eggs and add them slowly, then fold in the whipped cream and freeze.

To serve

Place the bavarois in the centre of the plate and top with the parfait.

Ingredients

Bavarois

250ml milk
3 eggs
125g caster sugar
25g gelatine
500g strawberry puree
300ml whipped double cream
250g fresh strawberries (cut in half)

Parfait

100g sugar
50ml water
1 egg
5 egg yolks
250ml double cream (whipped)

170
RAMSONS RESTAURANT

18 Market Place, Ramsbottom, Bury BL0 9HT

01706 825 070
www.ramsons-restaurant.com

Ramsons Restaurant is located in the West Pennine village of Ramsbottom, ten miles north of Manchester and just three minutes from junction one off the M66, so they are well situated for visitors to come and experience their 'foodie' philosophy of pan Italian cuisine.

Proprietor Chris Johnson believes that food should taste of what it is; that every element of a dish should be on the plate for a reason, so that the full flavours of each ingredient is available to be savoured and enjoyed. Chris says that food is a product of its environment (or terroir as the French call it), and Chris has spent a good part of the last quarter century trying to find farmers who appreciate and respect their terroir in order to produce some of the best cuisine around.

Despite serving Italian food, the restaurant is not Italian. Locals work alongside Durham born Chris Johnson, Maldives born Naseem and Tehran born Babak. Wherever they are from, they are united by a shared passion for the style of cuisine that can be found in Italy's finest restaurants and vineyards.

So why is the restaurant called 'Ramsons'?
Ramsons is the old English name for wild garlic, which thrives in the moist, cool climate of the West Pennine Valleys. At certain times of the year the aroma of garlic can be sensed all around Ramsbottom. And what better end to a country walk could there be than a dinner at Ramsons?

Ramsons Boss Chris Johnson has spent a good part of the last quarter century searching out farmers who appreciate and respect their terroir. His young team use these fine ingredients to produce some of the best cooking in Manchester

POACHED MACKEREL WITH LEMON PITH, PICKLED SHALLOTS AND AVOCADO PUREE

SERVES 2

🍷 *Riesling Rolly Gossman 2007*
Alsace

Ingredients

Mackerel
2 fresh mackerel fillets
1 tsp English mustard
1 tbsp olive oil

Pickled Shallots
shallots (finely sliced length ways)
50ml water
75gm caster sugar
1 lemon
50ml white wine vinegar

Avocado Puree
1 ripe avocado
2 tbsp olive oil
½ lemon (juiced)

Method

For the mackerel

Start by cutting the mackerel fillets into 8 pieces.

Boil a pan of water, add a pinch of salt and then remove it from the heat. Poach the mackerel gently in the water for about two minutes.

Remove, and whilst the mackerel is still warm, coat it with English mustard and a little olive oil.

For the pickled shallots

Heat the vinegar, water and sugar in a saucepan until boiling, then remove from the heat and add the shallots.

Leave the shallots to pickle for 15 minutes, allowing them to cool and then drain them.

Peel the lemon and then separate the white pith from the yellow skin using a sharp knife.

Cut the pith finely into strips and mix with the shallots. Discard the skin.

For the avocado puree

Peel the avocado and chop roughly. Then put the avocado in a jug with the olive oil and the juice from half a lemon and blend to a puree using a hand blender. Add seasoning to taste.

To serve

Serve the dish warm or cold as a starter; add salad leaves if you wish.

ROULADE OF CORN FED DUCK WITH SWEETCORN PUREE, PORT AND CARDONCELLI MUSHROOM SAUCE

SERVES 2

🍷 *Domaine de la Grand Cour Fleurie 2009 'Clos de la grand Cour'*

Ingredients

Roulade

1 large, corn fed duck breast (skinned and baby fillet removed)
2 large savoy cabbage leaves OR
3 large Swiss chard leaves
2 juniper berries (crushed)
salt and pepper

Puree

500g sweetcorn (fresh is best but use tinned if easier)
1 tsp of softened butter
salt and pepper

Sauce

100ml port
100ml red wine
200ml chicken stock
2 shallots (finely chopped)
2 large cardoncelli or chestnut mushrooms (finely chopped)
pinch of thyme
75g softened butter
salt and pepper

Method

For the roulade

Lay out a large piece of clingfilm on your work surface.

Blanch the cabbage or chard for 1 minute in boiling water and then cool in cold water. Lay the 2 savoy cabbage (or 3 chard) leaves on top of the film, with a slight overlap in the middle to ensure there are no gaps.

Season the leaves with salt and pepper and scatter over the crushed juniper berries.

Fold the duck breast length ways and place on top of the leaves then, using the clingfilm, wrap the leaves and duck into a tight sausage shape, ensuring that the leaves wrap all the way round the duck and that you leave at least 2 inches of clingfilm at each end.

Holding onto each end of the clingfilm, roll the roulade along the surface with a rolling pin action to tighten the roulade. Once you are happy that it is wrapped securely, tie off each end with a knot as close to the roulade as possible.

Place the roulade into boiling, salted water and turn down the heat.

Simmer the roulade for approximately 8 minutes for medium rare meat or 9-10 minutes if you prefer the meat medium.

Remove from the pan and set aside to rest for 5 minutes.

For the sauce

Add the port, wine and shallots to a saucepan.

Allow the liquid to reduce by 75% then add the chicken stock and reduce by half again.

While the mixture is reducing, sauté the mushrooms in a pan with a little butter.

Add the butter to the reduced liquid and whisk. This will give the sauce thickness and shine.

Finally stir in the sautéed mushrooms and season to taste.

For the puree

Take 300g of the sweetcorn and blitz it with a hand blender until smooth. Pass the puree through a fine sieve to remove any large lumps and smooth out the puree.

Warm the puree in a saucepan with the butter and season to taste.

To serve

Set down the puree in the middle of the plate and scatter some of the remaining sweetcorn on top and around the puree. Slice the roulade into 8 and place 4 slices per person on top of the puree. Finally, drizzle the sauce around the plate.

STEAMED CHERRY PUDDING WITH CHERRY BRANDY CUSTARD

SERVES 8

🍷 *Myriad Pinot Noir 2007 17.5%*
South Africa

Ingredients

Cherry Pudding

350g homemade cherry compote (See recipe)
120g butter
150g white bread crumbs
120g caster sugar
25g self raising flour
1 tsp bicarbonate of soda
3 whole eggs

Cherry Brandy Custard

5 egg yolks
500ml single cream
1 vanilla pod
70g white caster sugar
cherry brandy

Cherry Compote

500g cherries (stones removed)
250ml water
250g caster sugar

Method

For the cherry compote

Bring sugar and water to the boil and add cherries. Allow the mixture to reduce and go sticky for approx 25 minutes.

For the cherry brandy custard

Whisk eggs and sugar together.

Heat the cream with the vanilla and bring to the boil.

Add the cream to the egg and sugar mix, then transfer back to the pan and heat until thick.

Add cherry brandy to taste.

For the cherry pudding

Roughly chop up the cherry compote.

Butter the sides of your moulds (we use Dariole moulds) and add a small amount of cherry compote to cover the bottom of the moulds.

Put the cherry compote and butter in a pan and stir until the butter is melted and is well mixed. Then remove from the heat.

Mix all the dry ingredients in a bowl then add the cherry compote and butter to the dry mix.

Then add the eggs and mix well.

Fill each mould ¾ full with the sponge mixture and cover the mould with greaseproof paper, securing it with an elastic band.

Steam cook for 45 minutes for individual puddings or 1½ hours for a large pudding in a steam pan or bain-marie.

To serve

Turn out the pudding onto a plate.

Drizzle with the cherry brandy custard or serve in a separate jug.

Add a scoop of cherry sorbet or vanilla ice cream on the side of the pudding if you fancy!

180
ROOM
RESTAURANT

81 King Street, Manchester M2 4AH

0161 839 2005
www.roomrestaurant.com

Room is a unique, modern restaurant and cocktail bar located on King Street, in the centre of the commercial and shopping district of Manchester. An eclectic mix of antique and retro styles makes this a stunning place to enjoy a dining experience which offers cocktails, music and private dining until late. The 2 AA Rosette accredited, award-winning restaurant can cater for up to 120 diners and the bar for up to 80. Room is perfect for anything from a business lunch, to a shopper's retreat, or just to drop in for a cocktail or a coffee. At night, the restaurant comes alive with an evening brasserie atmosphere that you would expect within any cosmopolitan city, and Manchester is no exception.

Enjoy dinner for 2 in a quiet corner or take a window seat and enjoy your Room with a view.

The Private Dining Room, 'The Rose Room', can make your event intimate and secluded; whilst we can equally cater for larger parties such as weddings or christenings. Beautifully designed with contemporary décor, the Rose Room offers private dining for up to 58 or cocktail receptions for up to 100. With its very own bar this is an ideal room for total privacy. As well as this, on the last Monday of the month, Room hosts a monthly gathering for lovers of wine (and of course food!). Each evening includes a canapé reception followed by a 6 course dinner with expertly paired wines. Let Room play host to your party or event. The innovative menus, sophisticated surroundings and lots of flexibility will ensure your event will be one to remember.

Joining an exclusive club of just three other chefs in Manchester, Head Chef Pete Taylor has just secured Room the award of 2 AA Rosettes. His menu at Room is based on classic dishes, all produced with a contemporary twist.

KEDGEREE

SERVES 4

🍷 *Ad Hoc Wallflower Riesling, Larry Cherubino, Australia*

Ingredients

Risotto

200g Arborio risotto rice
50g good quality tandoori paste
50g white onion (diced)
200ml vegetable stock (hot)
50g parmesan cheese (grated)
100g Japanese bread crumbs (panko)
50g flour and 1 beaten egg – for bread crumbing

Smoked Haddock Ceviche

1 fillet smoked haddock (skinless and frozen for one hour, this will allow you to slice easier)
½ tsp white sugar
½ tsp sea salt
½ tsp harrisa paste
½ lime (juice and zest)
¼ tsp cumin
50ml extra virgin olive oil
2 cloves of garlic (minced)

Quail's Egg

8 quail eggs

Curried Pea Puree

200g frozen peas
50g curry paste
10 sprigs of coriander (picked and washed)
50g butter

Garnish

coriander cress

Method

For the risotto cakes

The mix makes 12 cakes, 3 per person.

Add a little olive oil, the diced onion and tandoori paste to a saucepan and cook for 5 minutes on a medium heat. Then add the Arborio rice and cook for a further 1 minute. Add the hot vegetable stock, one ladle at a time, until all stock is absorbed by the rice, and then add the grated parmesan. Taste and season if required and set the mixture aside until cold.

Once cold, shape the mixture into golf ball sized balls and place them into flour, egg and finally the breadcrumb mixture. Deep fry the risotto cakes for 3 minutes until golden, remove from the fryer onto kitchen roll and then serve right away.

For the smoked haddock ceviche

For the marinade, mix together white sugar, sea salt, harrisa paste, lime juice, cumin, olive oil and the remainder of the minced garlic in a bowl, then slice the haddock fillet finely and place it into the marinade. Set it aside for one hour.

For the curried pea puree

In a saucepan, place a little oil, some curry paste and frozen peas and cook for 25 minutes on a low heat.

Once cooked, add butter and place into the food processor, adding coriander. Puree until smooth and keep warm until needed.

For the quail's eggs

In a pan of simmering water, add the quail's eggs and cook for 2 ½ minutes. Once cooked, place the eggs into ice cold water. Leave for 2 minutes, and then peel gently.

To serve

Place three spoonfuls of the pea puree side by side onto the plate, and then sit the risotto cakes on top of the puree. Sit the marinated haddock on top of the risotto cakes. Finally, garnish the plate with the soft boiled quail's eggs and fresh coriander cress.

LAMB MOUSAKKA

SERVES 4

🍷 *Petit Verdot Pinotage Suikerbossie, South Africa*

Ingredients

Lamb

4 x 120g lamb rumps

Spiced Aubergine Caviar

¼ tsp cumin seeds
¼ tsp of coriander powder
¼ tsp paprika
1 small onion (diced)
2 aubergines (medium diced)
250ml pasata tomato sauce
1 tsp tomato puree
2 tbsp of sweet chilli sauce
50g sultanas
40g fresh mint (finely chopped)
40g fresh coriander (finely chopped)

Cucumber Raita

½ cucumber (seeded and diced)
100ml natural yoghurt
squeeze of lemon juice
2 sprigs of mint (washed and picked)

Feta Cheese Bon-Bons

100g of good feta cheese (room temperature)
50g fresh Japanese breadcrumbs (panko)
50g flour
1 egg (beaten)

Tomato Sauce

25ml white wine vinegar
25ml olive oil
1 clove garlic (minced)
25g sugar
remaining pasata tomato sauce

Method

For the spiced aubergine caviar

Add olive oil and the cumin, coriander powder and paprika to a saucepan and cook for 5 minutes on a medium heat, then add the onions and cook until soft. After this, add the diced aubergine and cook until golden. Add 100ml of pasata, tomato puree, sweet chilli sauce and sultanas and cook for a further 5 minutes before adding the fresh mint and coriander. Set aside until cool.

For the cucumber raita

Add salt to diced, seeded cucumber and set aside for 5 minutes, then wash the salt off with cold water. Place the cucumber onto a clean tea towel and squeeze to remove excess moisture, then mix it with lemon juice, mint and natural yoghurt.

For the feta cheese bon-bons

Soften the feta cheese with the back of a spoon and roll it into small, bon-bon sized balls and chill for 1 hour. Roll the feta bon-bons first in flour, then eggs and finally the breadcrumbs until completely coated. Deep fry bon-bons for 5 minutes until golden. Dry on kitchen paper and serve immediately.

For the tomato sauce

In a saucepan, fry the garlic on a medium heat for 3 minutes in olive oil. Add the remaining pasata, white wine vinegar and sugar. Simmer for 5 minutes and pass through a fine sieve. Keep the sauce warm until it is needed.

For the lamb

In a frying pan, heat olive oil and add the lamb to brown on both sides. Place the lamb into a 200°C oven until cooked to your liking, and then rest it in a warm place.

To serve

Place a little tomato sauce onto a plate and top it with the spiced aubergine mixture. Slice the lamb and place it on top of the mixture. Add a small amount of the cucumber raita and finally top with two bon-bons.

SUMMER PUDDING

SERVES 4

🍷 *Late harvest Sauvignon Blanc Echeverria, Chile*

Ingredients

Lemon Sponge Base

100g margarine
100g sugar
1 whole egg
100g self raising flour
2 tsp grated lemon zest
pinch of salt

Baverois

½ pint full cream milk
2 ½ gelatin leaves
4 egg yolks
100g sugar
200ml blackberry puree
½ pint double cream

Summer Jelly

2 leaves gelatin
100g sugar
25ml lemon juice
½ pint of water
8 strawberries
8 raspberries
8 blackberries

Method

For the lemon sponge base

Beat together the margarine and 100g of the sugar until light and fluffy, then slowly add the egg, flour, lemon zest and pinch of salt. Place onto a ½ inch thin baking tray and bake on 160°C for 12 minutes. When cooked, place to one side until cooled.

For the baverois

Add the milk to a saucepan and heat until simmering. While this is happening, place 2 ½ leaves of gelatin into cold water to soften. Put the egg yolks and 100g of the sugar into a bowl and whisk until light and fluffy and to this mixture add the hot milk, soaked gelatin leaves and blackberry puree. Then heat the mix gently to make a thick custard. Leave to cool.

Half whip the cream, add to the cold custard mixture and set aside in the fridge.

Using 4 mousse rings, 7cm x 3½cm deep and lined with clingfilm, cut out the sponge and top with the cream mixture. Chill for 2 hours.

For the summer jelly

Soak the remaining gelatin in water until soft. In a pan, bring to the boil a half pint of water then add the lemon juice, remaining sugar and the soaked gelatin. In four small espresso cups, place 2 of the strawberries, raspberries and blackberries, and pour over the jelly mixture once it has cooled. Leave in the fridge to chill.

To serve

Remove the sponge and cream from one of the mousse rings and place onto the centre of the plate. Sit the espresso cups filled with jelly in a little hot water to loosen them, and then turn out onto plate. Serve with clotted cream.

190
THE ROPE & ANCHOR

Paddock Lane, Dunham Massey, Altrincham WA14 5RP

0161 927 7901
www.thedeckersgroup.com

Lovingly renovated and restored in 2009/10, the Rope & Anchor has become a big part of life in beautiful Dunham Massey. Set amongst the rural landscape, this traditional English pub features fantastic home-made food and locally produced hand-pulled beers in exceptional surroundings.

Lee Mitchell and Sous chef Andy Chadderton lead a passionate team at the Rope & Anchor serving traditional favourites of prodigious quality. The team ensure the menu is both seasonal and varied through a frequently changing menu and daily blackboard specials.

Enjoy a bottle of wine from our carefully selected wine menu. If you would like any help making a choice, please ask one of our friendly members of staff who would be happy to help.

The Rope & Anchor features a large outdoor dining area including The Barn; a purpose built outdoor dining facility. The overhead heating and lovely fireplace allow you to enjoy outdoor dining, even when the English weather lets you down. The exterior includes a children's play area and a kitchen garden.

Inside the pub itself is superbly finished. Set over two floors, the interior is warm, welcoming, bright and airy. The ground floor bar is centrally located to provide quick and efficient service. The first floor bar and lounge provide a relaxed atmosphere to sit and enjoy the surroundings.

The changes to this pub were extensive, a labour of love. We are sure you will agree that it was worth the effort.

The Rope & Anchor features a large, outdoor dining area including The Barn; a purpose built outdoor dining facility. The overhead heating and lovely fireplace allow you to enjoy outdoor dining, even when the English weather lets you down

CHAR GRILLED SARDINES ON SOUR DOUGH TOAST, BANANA SHALLOT AND GARDEN HERB RELISH

SERVES 2

Arroyo de la vega white Rioja, Spain

Ingredients

Sardines
4 medium sized sardines (butterflied)
1 small sour dough cob/roll

Relish
25g banana shallot (finely diced)
5g basil
10ml Chardonnay vinegar
5g chives
5ml Coleman Dijon mustard
5g coriander
35g Heinz tomato ketchup
5g mint
5g garlic (peeled)
35ml rapeseed oil
5g tarragon
5g chervil
¼ lemon

Method

For the relish
Finely dice the shallots and roughly chop all the herbs, removing the stalks. Combine with all other ingredients, season and chill.

For the sardines
Ensure the sardines are clean and free from scales, then butter a metal tray with clarified butter and place on the sardines. Season and grill for 1-2 minutes, skin side up.

Slice the roll into two, remove the crust and toast on both sides.

To serve
Place sardines on top and dress with relish and fresh garden herbs.

COTE DE BOEUF, DRIPPING FRIED CHIPS, SPRING PODDED VEGETABLES, ROASTED VINE TOMATOES & BERNAISE SAUCE

SERVES 2

🍷 *Big Tree Bitter*
Dunham Massey Brewing Company

Ingredients

20oz rib of beef
2 medium sized Maris Piper potatoes
2 vine plum tomatoes
2 peeled banana shallots
100g medium button mushrooms
100g clarified butter

Spring Greens

6 spears fresh asparagus
50g sugar snap peas
50g fine beans
100g tender stem broccoli

Bernaise

100g butter (unsalted)
10g chervil
3g whole black pepper
20ml white wine vinegar
35g egg yolks pasteurised
¼ lemon
Maldon fine sea salt
10g tarragon

Method

For the bernaise

Start by placing the butter in a saucepan and heat until clarified. Then reduce the vinegar, tarragon stalks and peppercorns by half on the stove.

Whisk the yolks until doubled in size over a bain-marie, slowly whisking in the butter.

Season with salt, white pepper and lemon juice. If you need to correct the consistency, do it with warm water.

Add the chopped tarragon and chervil and it is ready to serve.

For the spring vegetables

Prepare the green vegetables to a similar size and shape as the chips.

For the entrée

Peel and wash the Maris Pipers, then par boil the potatoes and cut to the desired chip size. Once cooled, halve the tomatoes and shallots.

Take the beef, oil it and season well. Char grill both sides of the meat and finish in the oven at 195°C. Cook according to personal preference (5 minutes either side for medium rare) and rest well.

Whilst the joint is cooking, take the greens and mushrooms and sautee seperately in clarified butter, until al dente. Take the vine tomatoes and shallots, season and gently grill to caramelise. Fry the chips and serve.

To serve

Place the beef and accompaniments on to a wooden board or large serving plate. Serve the sauce separately.

DUNHAM MASSEY RHUBARB FOOL

SERVES 1

 Noble Taminga,
Australia

Method

For the rhubarb fool

Place the rhubarb, sugar, orange juice and enough water to cover the rhubarb in a medium pan. Boil rapidly until the rhubarb is soft.

In a bowl, fold the rhubarb into the whipped cream. Reserve a little rhubarb for decoration.

For the pavlova

Beat the egg whites and sugar to firm peaks.

Mix the corn flour, vanilla and vinegar to a paste, then slowly add the paste to the egg whites.

Pipe to required size onto a slip mat and cook at 100°C for 40 minutes.

To serve

Place a ring on top of the pavlova base and line with equally sized pieces of poached rhubarb. Spoon the fool mixture into the centre to fill and remove the ring. Take the little pavlovas, stick them together with the remaining fool mixture and place on top of the fool. Garnish with mint and poached rhubard pieces.

Ingredients

Rhubarb Fool

350g Dunham Massey rhubarb
55g caster sugar
1 orange (juice only)
water
150ml cream (whipped)

Pavlova

5ml malt vinegar
150g free range egg white
10ml vanilla flavouring
12g cornflour
300g caster sugar

200
SECOND FLOOR
RESTAURANT
AT HARVEY NICHOLS

21 Cathedral Street, Manchester M1 1AD

0161 828 8898
www.harveynichols.com

Stuart Thomson, head chef at the Second Floor Restaurant and Brasserie, Harvey Nichols Manchester, has been at the helm for 2 years, maintaining high standards and designing impressive menus using top quality and locally sourced produce.

Overlooking Exchange Square, the Harvey Nichols Second Floor Restaurant is an ideal haven to unwind with dinner and a fine wine while watching the world pass by. Firmly established as one of Manchester's top restaurants, the Second Floor Restaurant's Head Chef continues to delight guests with his mouth-watering and award-winning cuisine. Joining Harvey Nichols in 2004, Stuart was soon promoted to the position of Sous Chef, which he held for 2 ½ years before becoming head chef in 2009. He has also worked in the kitchens of The Lowry Hotel and Establishment of Manchester as well as The Balmoral and Cameron House Hotel in his native Scotland. Having stamped his own mark on the award winning restaurant, Stuart has now made a notable reputation for himself, helping the Second Floor to gain two AA Rosettes and an impressive list of reviews and accolades.

Overlooking Exchange Square, the Harvey Nichols Second Floor Restaurant is an ideal haven to unwind with dinner and a fine wine while watching the world pass by

PORTLAND CRAB

SERVES 4

🍷 *Grosset "Polish Hill" Riesling 2010*
Clare Valley Australia

Ingredients

Tomato Fondue

4 plum tomatoes (peeled and de-seeded)
1 banana shallot (finely chopped)
1 clove of garlic (finely chopped)
10g coriander (finely chopped)
6g salt

Crab Cake

400g white crab
100g brown crab
200g dry mash potato
100g tomato petals (finely diced)
20g chives (finely chopped)
5ml lemon juice
3g salt

Breadcrumbs

50g flour
2 eggs (beaten)
100g breadcrumbs

Crab Mayonnaise

200g picked white crab meat
80g mayonnaise
30g semi dried tomato petals
10g chives (finely chopped)
3g salt
5ml lemon juice

Avocado Puree

1 avocado
5ml lemon juice

Pickled Apple

2 Granny Smith apples
200ml Pickling liquor

Melba Toast

3 slice wholemeal bread

Method

For the tomato fondue

Cut the tomato flesh into 1 cm squares.

Sweat the shallot down with the salt until soft, without it colouring.

Then add the garlic and continue to cook for a couple of minutes.

Next add the tomato and cook until the tomato begins to soften but still retains its shape.

Hang in muslin for about 30 minutes in the fridge to cool.

When cold, mix in coriander.

For the crab cake

Mix the ingredients for the crab cake together and roll it up into 10g balls.

Then set aside in the freezer for 3 hours.

After this, roll each of the crab cakes in the flour followed by the egg then the breadcrumbs, and repeat once more with only the egg and flour.

Place the crab cakes back in the freezer.

To cook, deep fry at 160°C from frozen.

For the crab mayonnaise

Mix all the ingredients together and season with the salt and lemon juice.

For the avocado puree

Remove the skin and stone from the avocado and blitz in a food processor with a little lemon juice and some salt to season.

Take the puree and pass it through a fine sieve.

For the pickled apple

Peel the apples and dice into 1.5cm cubes, then cover with the pickling liquor for at least 2 hours.

For the melba toast

Toast the bread on both sides then remove the crusts and rub the untoasted side in a circular motion on a cold stainless steel bench to remove all the excess bread.

Cut the square of bread into sixteenths and lightly toast on the untoasted side until the bread triangles curl up.

To serve

Assemble as in the picture.

CHESHIRE LAMB

SERVES 4

Bandol, Domaine La Suffrene 2006
Provence France

Ingredients

Carrot and Cumin Puree

500g carrots (diced and peeled)
10g cumin seed (bashed)
300ml carrot juice
8g salt

Herb Crust

50g rosemary
20g parsley
300g fresh white bread crumbs, no crust
10g salt
10g butter

Lamb Breast

1 lamb breast (boned and rolled)
100g carrots (roughly chopped)
100g leeks (roughly chopped)
100g onion (roughly chopped)
10g thyme (chopped)
1 bay leaf
1 cloves of garlic (finely chopped)
2 sprigs of rosemary (finely chopped)
150ml vegetable stock

Lamb Sauce

cooking juices from the lamb
5g green olives (chopped)
2g flat leaf parsley (chopped)
5g tomato flesh (diced)
5g miniature capers

Method

For the carrot and cumin puree

Put all the ingredients in a large pan and bring them to the boil. Remove any foam that rises to the top. Once the carrots are cooked, place into a food processor and blend, and then pass through a fine sieve. Adjust the seasoning and chill. Reheat in a pan when needed.

For the herb crust

Blitz the herbs in a processor and separately blend the bread into fine crumbs, then add the herbs and the salt. Cook in a frying pan with some olive oil and foaming butter until the crumbs become dry, then chill.

For the lamb breast

Ask the butcher to remove the ribs from the breast and tie the lamb for roasting.

Mix all the ingredients and marinade for two days. Remove the lamb from the marinade and season, then rub a little vegetable oil on the surface. In a heavy based pan, sear the lamb on all sides to give an even, deep brown colour. Then remove the lamb and set to one side.

Add all the vegetables to the same pan and cook until golden brown, then place the lamb on top of the vegetables. Add the vegetable stock. Cover with aluminium foil then place in an oven, pre-heated to 160°C, for 3-4 hours. To check if it is cooked, scrape a fork over one end of the lamb and if it falls without any effort it will be cooked.

Pass the cooking liquor from the lamb through a fine sieve and reserve for the sauce. Leave to cool for 30 minutes then carefully lift the lamb out and place onto clingfilm and roll into long cylinders. Chill for a minimum of 3 hours.

Cut a thick slice of lamb and fry for 3 minutes on both sides. Brush with Dijon mustard and press the herb crumb against the mustard.

For the lamb sauce

Reduce the cooking juices until it can coat the back of a spoon. Heat the sauce when required, just before serving add the rest of the ingredients. Season with a little sherry vinegar.

To serve

Assemble as in picture.

MANUKA BRULEE

SERVES 4

 Schloss Gobelsburg Eiswein, Kamptal 2007
Austria

Ingredients

Lime Confit

10 limes
300g sugar
200ml lime cordial
10ml water

Manuka Brulee

12 free range egg yolks
85g sugar
85g Manuka honey
950ml cream
4 tbsp loose Manuka tea

Brown Sugar Jelly

120g soft dark brown sugar
250ml water
50ml brandy
5 gelatine leaves

Stock Syrup

150ml water
150g caster sugar

Apricot Puree

150g dried apricots
300ml stock syrup
1 orange

Honeycomb

325g sugar
50ml Manuka honey
125g glucose
60ml water
15g bicarbonate of soda

Method

For the lime confit

Segment the limes and pat dry with a kitchen towel.

Then add the water to the sugar and boil until a light caramel forms.

Next add the lime cordial and boil again.

Take it off the heat and add the segments, then allow to cool.

Place in an airtight jar, this will allow the lime confit to last a month.

For the manuka brulee

First boil the cream and Manuka tea, then mix the egg yolks and sugar together and pour the cream onto the eggs and sugar.

Pass through a muslin cloth and skin off the froth.

Pour into a 10cm x 14cm roasting tray and cook in an oven at 90°C for about 45 minutes.

For the brown sugar jelly

Soak the gelatine in cold water and leave to one side.

Then boil the sugar and water.

Next, take the gelatine, add it to the boiled sugar/water mix and whisk.

Add the brandy.

Pour into a tray lined with clingfilm and skim off the froth.

For the stock syrup

Mix the water and sugar together then bring to the boil.

For the apricot puree

Cover the dried apricots with stock syrup, then slice the orange and place it on top of the apricots to help keep them under the syrup.

Boil until soft then take out the orange slices.

Blitz in a thermo until smooth. Adjust the consistency with extra stock syrup if needed.

For the honeycomb

In a deep pan, boil all the ingredients except the bicarbonate of soda until a light caramel forms. Then add the bicarbonate of soda. Whisk quickly, then turn out onto greaseproof paper.

To serve

Spoon the brulee onto the plate. Arrange garnish of honeycomb, apricot puree, lime confit, brown sugar around the set brulee.

Hollingworth Lake

212
RELISH LARDER

AN INTRODUCTION FROM SHAUN TURNER OF THE NORTHWEST CHEF'S ASSOCIATION

As a Lancastrian living in Cheshire with a passion for foods from the Northwest region, it gives me great pleasure to write this introduction.

We are lucky to have many great chefs in our region and I am proud to shout about them, but without our farmers, growers and army of artisan producers, we wouldn't have the world class produce that we are lucky to have on our doorstep.

The Northwest region is arguably one of the most diverse food-producing areas in the country. Rural Cumbria is noted for its sheep & beef production, together with a well established artisan micro-producer base. Cheshire is the county of orchards, cereal, dairy and vegetable farming whilst Lancashire bridges the two with sheep and beef from its Bowland & Pennine regions; cheese and other dairy products from the green pastures between Chorley and Lancaster; and vegetables from the lowlands on both north and south sides of the Ribble and Mersey estuaries.

Many of the businesses listed in this regional larder have recently been recognised in the North West Fine Food Awards, announced at Nigel's Fantastic Food Show by Northwest Chefs' Association supporter and Michelin Star Chef, Nigel Haworth.

These regional awards saw nearly 400 products entered by 132 companies from across Cheshire, Cumbria, Greater Manchester, Lancashire and Merseyside.

What better way to celebrate the fantastic foods that we have in the region than to pay a visit to them and enjoy some of their great produce for yourselves.

Shaun Turner is Managing Director of Northwest Chefs' Association. A not for profit organisation set up to raise the profile of professional chefs and locals foods in the northwest region.

north west
chefs' association

BAKERY

BERRY FRESH BAKERY
Meadow Acre, Wrenbury Frith, Nantwich, CW5 8HN
01829 720433
www.berryfreshbakery.co.uk

Artisan produced jams, chutneys, marmalades and curds using locally grown produce wherever possible.

DEVONSHIRE BAKERY
1 High Street, Frodsham, Cheshire WA6 7AH
01928 731234
www.devonshire-bakery.co.uk

5th Generation bakers who have provided retail and wholesale bakery products to North Cheshire for over 100 years.

DOUGH 2B DIFFERENT
01254 388399
www.dough2bdifferent.co.uk

Dough 2b Different, The Artisan Bakery creates a continuously evolving range of artisan breads, seasonal desserts and patisserie.

GINGER BAKERS
Unit 6, Dockray Hall Industrial Estate, Kendal LA9 4RU
07990 541982
www.gingerbakers.co.uk

Ginger Bakers produce an inspiring array of cakes and bakes using the freshest ingredients, organic and locally sourced where possible, and always free range eggs.

GORGE' US
Gorge' Us, 7 Church Road, Bebington, Wirral CH63 7PG
01516 6448133
www.gorge-us.co.uk

Gorge'Us is a small, cosy coffee shop, situated in Bebington Village, a 5 minute walk away from the historical village of Port Sunlight, and is owned and run by Ceri Newton.

BEVERAGES

BOWLAND BEER COMPANY
Bashall Town, Clitheroe, Lancashire.
01200 443592
www.bowlandbrewery.com

The Bowland Brewery is situated close to the exact geographical centre of the United Kingdom in the beautiful Forest of Bowland. Since April 2003, the brewery has produced hand-crafted real ales using the finest Maris Otter malted barley and full-flower hops.

D.BYRNE & CO
12 King Street, Clitheroe, Lancashire BB7 2EP
01200 423152
www.dbyrne-finewines.co.uk

D. Byrne & Co is a family owned and run award winning fine wine merchants. The family have between them over 80 years experience in the business.

DUNHAM MASSEY BREWING COMPANY
100 Oldfield Lane, Dunham
Massey, Altrincham WA14 4PE
0161 929 0663
www.dunhammasseybrewing.co.uk

Dunham Massey Brewing Company is a small family run craft brewery located on National Trust land in the town of Dunham Massey.

FRODSHAM BREWERY
Lady Heyes Craft Centre, Kingsley
Road, Frodsham, Cheshire, WA6 6SU
01928 787917
www.frodshambrewery.co.uk

Frodsham microbrewery is a small, friendly, craft based brewery and shop. Barrie and his wife Hazel run it, with assistance from Paula in sales and Ken, the drayman.

BEVERAGES

MAWSONS TRADITIONAL DRINKS
Unit 11a New Line Industrial Estate, Bacup,
Lancashire, OL13 9RW
01706 874448
www.mawsons.co.uk

*Offering sarsaparilla, dandelion and burdock and cream
soda, Mawsons is bringing back the tastes of yesteryear
using skills honed over several generations.*

PECKFORTON HILLS WATER
1 Rosebank, High Street, Tattenhall, CH3 9PR
01829 770381
www.peckforton.co.uk

*Locally sourced, bottled Cheshire spring water, from
the beautiful Peckforton hills. We are committed to
environmental sustainability and serving our customers
with the highest possible quality products.*

COOKED MEAT, PIES AND PATES

CRANSTONS QUALITY BUTCHERS
Ullswater Road, Penrith, Cumbria, CA11 7EH
01768 868680
www.cranstons.net

*Cranstons Quality Butchers was established in 1914 by
the current director's Great Uncle, Stanley Cranston, who
developed a reputation for selling the top quality meat
products in the Eden Valley from his horse and cart.*

DIGGLES LTD
56 North Road, Lancaster, Lancashire LA1 1LT
01524 62060
www.diggles.co.uk

*Diggles sell a wide range of fresh products including
traditional cooked meats and hot and cold pies.*

HOME 2 HOME DINING
78, Runcorn Rd, Moore,
Warrington, Cheshire, WA4 6TZ
01925 740561
www.home2homedining.co.uk

*Thomas and Esther produce a wide range of foods, such as
their award winning Pâté, potted beef, frozen ready meals.*

THE LANCASHIRE PASTY COMPANY
784 Whalley New Road, Blackburn, Lancashire,
BB1 9BA
01254 610895
www.lancashirepastycompany.co.uk

*After trading for 26 years as Wood's Craft Bakery, the Wood
family are now concentrating on one of their best selling
lines, The Lancashire pasty, hence their new baby The
Lancashire Pasty Company!*

THE MAFEKING BILTONG COMPANY LTD
30 Sandy Lane, Macclesfield, Cheshire, SK10 4RJ
07704 339 777
www.mafekingbiltong.co.uk

*Award-winning biltong made in Macclesfield with Cheshire
beef.*

CONFECTIONERY

CHESHIRE CHOCOLATES
22 Brookside Lane, High Lane, Stockport, Cheshire,
SK6 8HL
01663 763309
www.cheshirechocolates.co.uk

Chocolates that are freshly made in small batches using the finest chocolate, imported from Belgium. Using their own ganache fillings, made with fresh fruit purees, oils and whenever possible, locally sourced ingredients.

CHOCOLATEHOUSE 1657
54 Branthwaite Brow, Kendal,
Cumbria, LA9 4TX 01539 740702
www.chocolatehouse1657.co.uk

An Aladdin's cave of chocolates and gifts plus a chocolate restaurant where you can enjoy chocolate drinks, gateaux and ice creams.

KOKONOIR CHOCOLATES
41 The Boulevard, Broughton, Chester
(website says Flintshire, Wales), CH4 0SN.
01244 534352
www.kokonoir.com

Jo and Toby Beevers started Kokonoir in Broughton from a shared love of how chocolates should taste. Their chocolates are all handcrafted, using traditional artisan skills to guarantee a fresh, delicious taste.

THE OLD FIRE STATION CHOCOLATE SHOP
52–54 High Street, Tarporley, Cheshire, CW6 0AG
01829 733736
www.firestationchocolateshop.co.uk

Handmade Freudenberg truffles, chocolate animals and a range of fudges are made on the premises at this old fire station in the village of Tarporley. Whatever the occasion we have chocolates to suit.

THE PASTRY KING
Alderley Road, Chelsford, SK11 9AP
01565 818228
www.thepastryking.co.uk

The Pastry King is a bakery that produces fantastic quality desserts, chocolates and cakes as they are ordered. From dinner parties to wedding cakes, they can help you.

SIMON DUNN CHOCOLATIERS
Alderley Road, Wilmslow, Cheshire SK9 1JX
01625 529105
www.simondunnchocolates.co.uk

With over 25 years of experience, you can expect superb quality. All of their chocolates are made in-store by expert chocolatiers.

DAIRY

CHESHIRE FARM ICE CREAM
Drumlan Hall Farm, Newton lane,
Tattenhall, Chester Cheshire, CH3 9NE
01829 770995
www.cheshirefarmicecream.co.uk

Produced on the farm, Cheshire Farm's award winning Real Dairy Ice Cream is made using fresh whole milk and fresh cream. Only the finest ingredients are carefully selected and used.

DELAMERE DAIRY
Delamere Dairy Ltd, Yew Tree Farm, Bexton
Lane, Knutsford, Cheshire, WA16 9BH
01565 750528
www.delameredairy.co.uk

Roger and Liz Sutton named their dairy after Cheshire's beautiful Delamere Forest where they started their first herd with just three goats.

BURT'S CHEESE
L & M Business Park, Norman
Road, Altrincham, WA14 4EP
077709 394292
www.burtscheese.com

Burt's Blue Cheese is a semi-soft blue cheese made in Altrincham, Cheshire, with quality milk sourced from a local dairy for a richer flavour. It is made in small vats, making each cheese a labour of love.

TIRESFORD GUERNSEY GOLD
Tiresford Farm, Tarporley, Cheshire, CW6 9LY
01829 734080
www.tggcheshireyogurt.co.uk

A first generation family farm based on the outskirts of the picturesque village of Tarporley in Cheshire.

FARMSHOPS

EDDISBURY FRUIT FARM
Yeld Lane, Kelsall, Cheshire, CW6 0TE
08450 941023
www.eddisbury.co.uk

Eddisbury Fruit Farm was established in 1936 by Leslie Haworth. The farm grows over 20 varieties of apples available in season for pick your own. They manufacture over 20 different single and blended varieties of apple juice using soft fruits grown on the farm.

THE HOLLIES FARM SHOP
Little Budworth, Cheshire, CW6 9ES
01829 760414
www.theholliesfarmshop.co.uk

Situated in the heart of Cheshire, The Hollies Farm Shops draw on half a century of experience, selling the best fresh produce from the best local producers.

RESTBURY FARM SHOP
The Village, Prestbury, Cheshire, SK10 4DG
01625 820035
www.prestburysfarmshop.co.uk

Located in the picturesque village of Prestbury, The Prestbury Farm Shop is one of the finest purveyors of quality local produce in the county.

RIVERSIDE ORGANIC
Shipbrook Hill Farm, Manor Lane,
Whatcroft, Northwich, Cheshire, CW9 7RH
01606 46258
www.riversideorganic.com

Riverside Organic is a family run farm, farm shop and cafe in Whatcroft, just out side Davenham in Cheshire. They started selling direct to the public in 2005 and now boast a large range of organic produce including beef, lamb, chicken, eggs, herbs, veg and fruit.

FISH

FURNESS FISH & GAME
Moor Lane, Flookburgh, Grange-
over-Sands, Cumbria, LA11 7LS
01539 559544
www.morecambebayshrimps.com

A family business started by the owner Les Salisbury who has been fishing for shrimps since he was a lad, going out on the horse and cart.

SOUTHPORT POTTED SHRIMPS
66 Station Road, Banks Village,
Southport, Lancs, PR9 8BB
01704 229266
www.pottedshrimp.co.uk

Southport Potted Shrimps was founded in 1980 by James Peet, a shrimp fisherman for 25 years, whose family has been involved in the local shrimp industry for over four generations.

SOUTHPORT SEAFOODS
11 Shellfield Road, Marshside,
Southport, PR9 9US 01704 505822
www.southportseafoods.co.uk

Southport Seafoods opened in 1992 and since that date they have provided the finest quality potted shrimps which are available throughout the U.K.

MEAT

A. PICTON & SONS
Highfield Farm Shop, Waterworks
Lane, Winwick, Warrington, WA2 8TB
www.highfieldfarmshop.co.uk

Highfield farm shop produces high quality, home reared beef, lamb and pork, as well as potatoes, fruit, vegetables, eggs, jams and chutneys

CLARKES OF LYTHAM
Market Buildings, Lytham, Lancashire, FY8 5LS
01253 736687
www.clarkesoflytham.co.uk

Award winning Lancashire butchers, selling finest quality sausages, meat and poultry.

DALES TRADITIONAL BUTCHERS
2 Market Street, Kirkby Lonsdale, LA6 2AU
015242 71278
www.dalesbutchers.co.uk

Mark Duckworth runs Dales Traditional Butchers and has been in the trade for over 25 years. They are based in Kirkby Lonsdale and produce a range of award winning pies and sausages as well as being an online butchers.

H CLEWLOW BUTCHERS
8 Pepper Street, Nantwich, Cheshire. CW5 5AB
01270 625366
www.clewlows.co.uk

*Traditional Butchers Shop since 1929, using locally sourced,
high quality stock from local farms.*

THE REAL LANCASHIRE BLACK PUDDING COMPANY
Unit 4, Waterside Industrial Estate,
Haslingden, Lancashire, BB4 5EN
01706 231029
www.reallancashireblackpuddings.co.uk

*The Bury Type of Black Pudding is the most favoured and
considered the most traditional of all the Black Puddings.*

PRESERVES, RELISHES, HONEY & PUDDINGS

ADESSO HEALTH LOVING
Unit 1, Railway Street Industrial Estate, Froxmer
Street, Gorton, Greater Manchester, M188EF
0161 231 0088
www.adessofoods.co.uk

*Adesso takes great pride in creating Ambient Marinades,
Dips and Drizzles from only the finest ingredients.*

FIND INSPIRATION IN FOOD
The Old Post Office, 1a Oak Road, Hooton, CH66 7NP
01513 273831
www.findinspirationinfood.co.uk

Homemade, luxury preserves.

PARKERS PRESERVES
Summerseat, Blackburn, Lancashire, BL9 5PN
01706 281 993
www.parkerspreserves.co.uk

*Homemade, using only the freshest fruits and vegetables,
with no artificial colouring , flavourings, or preservatives.*

REEDY'S NATURALLY
Unit 9, Elder Court, Shadsworth Business
Park, Blackburn, Lancashire BB1 2EQ
01254 691 754
www.reedys.co.uk

*Delicious luxury jams, marmalades and savory condiments
handmade in the heart of Lancashire.*

SMOKED FOODS

THE CHESHIRE SMOKEHOUSE
Vost Farm, Morley Green, Wilmslow, Cheshire, SK9 5NU
01625 548499
www.cheshiresmokehouse.co.uk

*In recent years The Cheshire Smokehouse has earned a
national reputation for the quality of its range of fine foods.*

PORT OF LANCASTER SMOKEHOUSE
West Quay, Glasson Dock, Lancaster, LA2 0DB
01524 752168
www.polsco.co.uk

*Established over thirty years ago, the Port of Lancaster
Smokehouse has retained and maintained the traditional
methods of preparing and curing fish and meats of all kinds.*

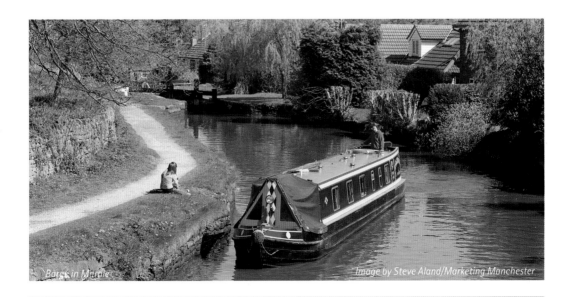

Barge in Marple

Image by Steve Aland/Marketing Manchester

Rochdale

1539 RESTAURANT & BAR

The Racecourse, Chester CH1 2LY
01244 304611
www.restaurant1539.co.uk

ALDERLEY RESTAURANT

Alderley Edge Hotel, Macclesfield
Road, Alderley Edge, Cheshire SK9 7BJ
01625 583 033
www.alderleyedgehotel.com

AUMBRY

2 Church Lane, Prestwich, Manchester M25 1AJ
0161 798 5841
www.aumbryrestaurant.co.uk

CITY CAFÉ AT THE MINT HOTEL

1 Auburn Street, 1 Piccadilly Place, Manchester M1 3DG
0161 242 1000
www.citycafe.co.uk

THE ELEPHANT AND CASTLE

608 Bury Road, Bamford, Rochdale OL11 4AU
01706 642 277
www.theelephantandcastle.co.uk

EVUNA

227–229 Deansgate, Manchester, M3 4EW
0161 819 2752
www.evuna.com

JEM & I

1C School Lane, Didsbury, Manchester M20 6RD
0161 445 3996
www.jemandirestaurant.co.uk

JODRELL BANK

The Planet Pavillion Cafe, Jodrell Bank Discovery Centre,
University of Manchester, Macclesfield SK11 9DW
01477 571 321
www.themoderncaterer.co.uk

MALMAISON MANCHESTER

Piccadilly, Manchester M1 1LZ
0161 278 1000
www.malmaison.com

THE MARK ADDY

Stanley Street, Salford, Manchester M3 5EJ
0161 832 4080
www.markaddy.co.uk

MARKET RESTAURANT

104 High Street, Manchester M4 1HQ
0161 834 3743
www.market-restaurant.com

MICHAEL CAINES AT ABODE CHESTER

Grosvener Road, Chester CH1 2DJ
01244 347 000
www.abodehotels.co.uk

MICHAEL CAINES AT ABODE MANCHESTER

107 Piccadilly, Manchester M1 2BD
0161 200 5678
www.abodehotels.co.uk

NUTTERS RESTAURANT

Edenfield Road, Norden, Rochdale OL12 7TT
01706 650 167
www.nuttersrestaurant.co.uk

THE PEACOCK ROOM

Crimble Lane, Bamford, Rochdale OL11 4AD
01706 368 591
www.thedeckersgroup.com

THE PLOUGH & FLAIL

Paddock Hill, Mobberley, Cheshire WA16 7DB
01565 873 537
www.thedeckersgroup.com

RAMSONS RESTAURANT

18 Market Place, Ramsbottom, Bury BL0 9HT
01706 825 070
www.ramsons-restaurant.com

ROOM RESTAURANT

81 King Street, Manchester M2 4AH
0161 839 2005
www.roomrestaurants.com

THE ROPE & ANCHOR

Paddock Lane, Dunham Massey, Altrincham WA14 5RP
0161 927 7901
www.thedeckersgroup.com

SECOND FLOOR RESTAURANT AT HARVEY NICHOLS

21 Cathedral Street, Manchester M1 1AD
0161 828 8898
www.harveynichols.com

MORE QUALITY RECIPE BOOKS
AVAILABLE FROM THIS PUBLISHER

Relish North East – From the bustling city life in Newcastle, to the multitude of sleepy, rural villages, the North East has something for everyone. An introduction from the North east's best known chef, Terry Laybourne, kicks off this culinary adventure through a rich and diverse region, with many varied recipes for you to try at home including a selection from the North East's two Masterchef finalists, John Calton and David Coulson, plus many others from award-winning chefs across the region.

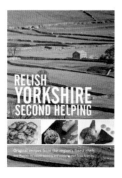

Relish Yorkshire Second Helping – The latest edition of relish Yorkshire features a foreword by celebrity chef Tessa Bramley, and returns to the county with all new recipes from Yorkshire's greatest chefs; Michelin Starred James McKenzie from The Pipe and Glass and Steve Smith from The Burlington, plus Richard Allen from The Fourth Floor at Harvey Nichols and many, many more. Relish Yorkshire: Second Helping is a must have for any hearty food lover with true Yorkshire pride.

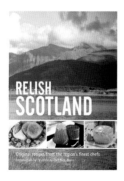

Relish Scotland – With over 300 Pages of Scotland's finest recipes, this book takes you on an epic journey from Edinburgh to Glasgow, across to Aberdeen and then up to the Highlands and Islands, through rugged landscapes and beautiful cities. An introduction from TV celebrity chef Nick Nairn prepares the palate for recipes from nationally acclaimed restaurateurs such as Tom Kitchin, Martin Wishart and Geoffrey Smeddle. With breathtaking pictures of the views and venues, Relish Scotland promises to make for fascinating reading for both foodies and tourists alike.

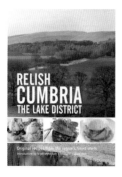

Relish Cumbria – Over 50 mouth-watering exclusive recipes for you to try at home from some of Cumbria's finest Country House Hotels and acclaimed restaurants including Nigel Mendham at The Samling, Russell Plowman at Gilpin Lodge Hotel and Andrew McGeorge at Rampsbeck Country House Hotel. Packed with innovative recipes and stunning photography to match the stunning landscape, Relish Cumbria is certain to make a fantastic addition to any cook's library.

Relish Publications – Relish Publications are an independent publisher of exclusive regional recipe books, featuring only the best and brightest critically acclaimed chefs and the venues at which they work, all of which showcased with superb photography. They also work with some chefs individually to produce bespoke publications tailored to their individual specifications. Since 2009, Relish has fostered a national presence, while maintaining friendly, personalised service that their small but highly professional team prides themselves on.

For more information about current and future Relish books, as well as information about the chefs and restaurants featured in them, visit www.relishpublications.co.uk

Proud sponsors of

RELISH
PUBLICATIONS